THE READING CLUB

A Guide to a Literacy Intervention Program for Reluctant Readers in Spanish and English

Kathryn Henn-Reinke

ScarecrowEducation
Lanham, Maryland • Toronto • Oxford
2004

Published in the United States of America
by ScarecrowEducation
An imprint of The Rowman & Littlefield Publishing Group, Inc.
4501 Forbes Boulevard, Suite 200, Lanham, Maryland 20706
www.scalescroweducation.com

PO Box 317
Oxford
OX2 9RU, UK

British Library Cataloguing in Publication Information Available

Library of Congress Cataloging-in-Publication Data

Henn-Reinke, Kathryn.
    The reading club : a guide to a literacy intervention program for reluctant
readers in Spanish and English / Kathryn Henn-Reinke.
        p. cm.
    Includes bibliographical references and index.
    ISBN 1-57886-168-3 (pbk. : alk. paper)
    1. Reading—Remedial teaching—United States. 2. Group reading—United
States. 3. Education, Bilingual—United States. I. Title.
LB1050.5.H345   2004
372.43—dc2   2004008972

♾™ The paper used in this publication meets the minimum requirements of
American National Standard for Information Sciences—Permanence of
Paper for Printed Library Materials, ANSI/NISO Z39.48-1992.
Manufactured in the United States of America.

To JAR, my constant companion and support,
and to JCCR and JGKR,
who entertain me and make me so proud.

CONTENTS

INTRODUCTION

This guide outlines an intervention program for students who struggle in their literacy development. The Reading Club/El Club de Lectura may be offered in English and/or Spanish. (The bilingual schools featured in this guide refer to the program as *El Club de Lectura*. Because many schools that may adopt the program are not bilingual schools, the program will be referred to as *The Reading Club* in this book.) It is designed for small groups of four, but may be used with smaller groups to provide more individualized instruction. The intervention program described in this guide is managed by trained educational assistants, although it can be conducted by classroom teachers or reading specialists.

School districts are required to have all students reading at grade level by the year 2012 (NCLB, 2001). Such an exceedingly lofty goal cannot be achieved without powerful intervention programs. The Reading Club provides a large number of its students with grade-level literacy skills within a single academic year. It addresses all the reading components of the Reads First Initiative (2001), including phonemic awareness, phonics, vocabulary, fluency, and comprehension. In addition, there is a well-developed emphasis on strategy development and assessment of student progress. The format of the lessons involves daily thirty-minute intervention sessions that complement but do not replace classroom literacy instruction.

The Reading Club lends itself to the establishment of partnerships between schools and universities. This book reflects such a partnership, with the university providing inservice training for the educational assistants and the schools providing opportunities for preservice teachers to observe in their classrooms. When two or more schools within a single district use The Reading Club, they effectively conserve resources by combining inservice sessions.

Two bilingual schools in Milwaukee have fully operational Club de Lectura programs. Many of their experiences are featured throughout this guide. The principals at both schools have assigned educational assistants to work exclusively in El Club de Lectura for most of their assigned time. Each assistant has her own teaching space where books, materials, and records are easily accessible.

The Hayes Two-Way Bilingual School implemented El Club de Lectura in 1997 and has used it as an intervention program ever since. Struggling students in first to third grade have generally been included in the sessions, though when staffing was available fourth and fifth grades were also included. At Hayes, children develop language and literacy skills in both Spanish and English. They learn to read and write first in their native language, while acquiring oral skills in the second language. Special emphasis is given to integrating science and technology across the curriculum using challenging, active, and cooperative learning activities.

James Whitcomb Riley Elementary School is a bilingual/bicultural school located on the southeast side of Milwaukee. The school has a student population of approximately 650 students, housed on two campuses. Students in kindergarten to fifth grade attend the main campus, while the Headstart and K–4 students attend school at the second campus. This multicultural school community embraces the concepts of high academic standards supported by a rigorous, integrated curriculum. J. W. Riley, which initiated El Club de Lectura in 2003, was the recipient of the Title I Distinguished School Award in 2000. The first chapter of this book provides an overview of the rationale and philosophy of The Reading Club. Chapter 2 describes the components of typical lessons in the program. Chapter 3 emphasizes assessment and monitoring of student progress, and chapter 4 provides an overview of possible inservice sessions for educational assistants who work with children in The Reading Club. The fifth chapter focuses specifically on the development of reading strategies, and the sixth and final chapter discusses the development of criteria to exit students from the program. These chapters are followed by appendixes outlining plans that are used for including kindergarten, fourth-grade, and fifth-grade students in The Reading Club; sample testing materials; sample Word Works materials; student self-assessment forms; and sample inservice materials.

It takes a principal with insight and courage to implement new programs in a school. Andrew Patterson, first as principal of the Hayes Two-Way Bilingual School and then as principal of the James Whitcomb Riley Elementary School, is that principal. I would like to thank him for the opportunity to work with both schools and for lending the kind of support that has made both programs successful.

As the new administrator of the Hayes Two-Way Bilingual School, Yolanda Hernández continues to support El Club de Lectura in the energetic manner with which she approaches everything. Her door is always open and she lets me barge in whenever I have a question. Sol María Colón has become the educational assistant who is expert in working with students in El Club de Lectura. She consistently goes above and beyond the call of duty in meeting the needs of her students. She had the courage to make a presentation with me about El Club de Lectura at the Wisconsin Association of Bilingual Education Conference, though it nearly scared her to death. Many other educational assistants have taught in El Club de Lectura: Roselia (now a teacher with a master's degree), Virgilio, Lymari, Julia, Jannette (now a teacher), Diana, Myrta, Liliana (now also a teacher), Rosa, and Phyllis have been extremely dedicated.

María Gonzalez de Nuñez allowed me to pilot El Club de Lectura in her second-grade classroom during my sabbatical in 1996. María, Patricia Mockus, and Lorena Gueny were my biggest supporters in getting the program up and running. The late Margaret Werner, as principal of Forest Home Avenue Elementary School, always gave me the leeway to work with these three incredible teachers, my former students.

Of course, one can never complete a book without support from home and family. John, Jonathan, and Jayme make it all possible.

❶

OVERVIEW OF THE READING CLUB

Nearly all children can become literate if given the opportunity and the necessary attention, although some require more individualized and specialized attention than others. These children are the focus of this guide. Not only have their peers passed them by, but also their schools are under increasing pressure (*No Child Left Behind,* 2001) to get them reading at grade level. This federal legislation mandates that children be reading at grade level by the end of the primary grades. Therefore, many schools are searching for effective literacy intervention programs that will successfully and significantly raise the literacy skills of their struggling readers. The Reading Club has supported many students in reaching grade-level expectations and has done so for most primary students within a single academic year.

The Reading Club promises a gentler, yet successful way to work with struggling readers in English and/or Spanish. This approach is designed for districts that have many struggling readers but insufficient resources to provide individualized support to students who face significant challenges to literacy development. It draws from the format of the Reading Recovery Model (Clay, 1985), as well as experts in the development of reading and writing skills and strategies, such as Cunningham (1995), Fountas and Pinnell (1996), Avery (1999), and Routman (2000).

The intention of The Reading Club is to start at the instructional level of the students in terms of literacy development but then to move them forward as quickly as possible. The level of the books being read, word analysis work, and student writing are continually evaluated. As soon as students reach a comfort zone with the materials at a specific level, they are nudged forward and given slightly more challenging work.

Most students in The Reading Club are significantly behind their classmates and need to make accelerated progress to reach grade-level expectations. Therefore, the lessons must be very concise and focused. Only four components are included in a Reading Club lesson (new book reading, word works, rereading of "old" books, and writing). Use of additional materials, such as worksheets and art projects, is discouraged as they may detract attention from developing the critical reading base that is being established in The Reading Club.

Every aspect of The Reading Club is centered on the premise that the most important goal is to teach children to read for meaning. Students focus on phonemic awareness and phonics during the word works component of the lessons, but the emphasis is on using these skills to improve fluency and comprehension of text. Students learn reading strategies that also can be used to facilitate getting meaning from print. Students write on a daily basis, and the relationship between reading and writing is made clear.

The goal of The Reading Club is to exit students from the program within one academic year. This has been the case for most students in The Reading Club (Henn-Reinke, 2001). Students remain in the program until they are very successfully able to complete grade-level literacy work in their dominant language. Attitudes toward reading and writing generally become more and more positive as students gain expertise and confidence in their literacy skills. Therefore, the emergence of greater self-esteem may be the first indicator of student progress.

It must also be stressed that The Reading Club is not an end in itself. The most successful students come from classrooms where the teachers communicate regularly with the educational assistants about the children's work. They support the work of The Reading Club and help students make connections between the learning experiences in both venues.

There are two significant differences in The Reading Club model relative to existing models. The first is that instead of one-on-one sessions, children meet in small groups of four. This is especially necessary in schools that have large numbers of students in need of assistance. Secondly, in this approach students meet with an educational assistant rather than a reading specialist. Reading specialists very often do not exist in the numbers needed. Working with educational assistants necessitates a rigorous and ongoing inservice agenda to build background regarding stages of literacy development, processes of becoming literate, strategy development, etc. Of course, schools that have more resources may opt to have one or more teachers conducting Reading Club sessions rather than educational assistants.

Schools will need to decide on the level of commitment they are willing to make to The Reading Club. Both schools featured in this guide trained two full-time educational assistants, and their sole responsibility was to meet with Reading Club students in first through third grades. (Two bilingual schools in Milwaukee, Wisconsin, will be highlighted in this guide. Both schools have successfully implemented the Club de Lectura program in English and in Spanish.) One educational assistant worked with children in English, and the other worked with children in Spanish at each school. Other schools have two or more educational assistants who dedicate a portion of their day to teaching Reading Club sessions. Our experience suggests that the most effective programs have clearly established guidelines for scheduling, selection of students, work spaces, and material access.

Students who generally participate in The Reading Club are those who lag significantly behind their peers but who seem to demonstrate the greatest potential for success in an intervention program. They are not students who have diagnosed special academic or emotional needs or who demonstrate serious behavioral challenges in the classroom. Educational assistants are generally not trained in addressing these specialized needs, and such students are often already receiving special education support. The Reading Club strives to address the needs of children who only need specialized attention in literacy development. Very often the children we've worked with had not yet developed a clear sense of the reading process. With the extra support, most students reached grade-level proficiency in literacy development within eight to nine months.

Schools that are new to The Reading Club concept may opt to begin with first-grade students who are significantly lagging behind their peers in literacy development. The number of identified students and the resources available within the school will determine the number of groups of students and the number of educational assistants to be devoted to the program. In our experience, it often took longer for first-grade students to begin showing significant progress, but once they began to understand the reading process, they made very steady gains. Second-grade students, on the other hand, generally demonstrated a very different pattern. These students had been exposed to an additional year of literacy experiences. They understood bits and pieces of what reading and writing entailed, but they had not yet internalized them to form a cohesive understanding of literacy. Their progress in The Reading Club was often much more dramatic and immediate than for the first-graders. Therefore, if resources are available, schools may wish to consider beginning with first grade and adding second grade (and possibly third grade) once the schedule and format for first grade are firmly established.

It has been suggested that The Reading Club may prove beneficial for second-semester kindergarten students. Some preliminary teaching plans for such an addition are presented in appendix A. We have also worked with students in third through fifth grades. Very often they were either transfer students or students who were recently arrived from Spanish-speaking countries and lacked academic skills in their first language. They received initial intervention services in Spanish. After they improved in their Spanish skills *and* had gained a fair level of oral proficiency in English, they also benefited from Reading Club sessions in English. A pilot project for fourth and fifth grades can be found in appendixes B and C, respectively. In this design, students received literacy instruction through the content area of social studies. This design seemed very promising, but further research remains to be done on its effectiveness.

SELECTION OF EDUCATIONAL ASSISTANTS

Careful selection of educational assistants to work with Reading Club groups cannot be overemphasized. There are some preliminary qualifications that schools may wish to take into consideration in determining who will be selected. Educational assistants must have very well developed literacy skills in the language of instruction. Secondly, we have found it of critical importance to select educational assistants with impeccable attendance records. Inconsistent work with The Reading Club groups due to attendance irregularities has *always* resulted in much lower progress for the children. Thirdly, these children already feel anxious because they are often working at their frustration level in the classroom. Therefore, it is critical to select educational assistants who will be firm yet positive and who will hold high expectations but provide the emotional and academic support necessary for students to reach their goals.

SELECTION OF STUDENTS

After the numbers of groups/grade levels to be served have been determined, it will be time to select the students for each group. An initial screening process will determine whether or not the students warrant membership in The Reading Club. Teachers may be asked to identify the four lowest-performing students in the class. The schools in Milwaukee, Wisconsin, that already use The Reading Club program have opted to eliminate students with identified special needs from membership in The Reading Club, because they are already receiving additional support.

Principals and reading specialists may wish to collaborate with teachers in selecting students. When this process is based on current assessment data and teacher observation, it helps ensure that selection is based on documented needs and not on other motivations. It is also advisable to avoid placing students with pronounced behavioral or emotional challenges in The Reading Club. The educational assistants are not generally equipped to deal with these issues in addition to challenges in literacy development.

Initially, there may be a temptation to put more than four students in each group. In some cases, the educational assistants may have previously worked with larger groups in the classroom, and teachers may wish to have them continue working with the same number of children.

In other instances, classroom teachers may have a large number of struggling readers and wish to make certain they all receive as much additional support as possible. However, even in groups of four it can be a challenge to meet the needs of all the students. In groups larger than four, the students who require the highest level of individualized attention become lost within the group, thereby defeating the very purpose of The Reading Club.

Parents are notified of their child's selection for participation in The Reading Club and are encouraged to visit literacy sessions. (A sample parent letter can be found in appendix G.) Teachers are encouraged to include information about the child's performance, including work samples, in parent-teacher conference sessions.

Many students who begin The Reading Club in September are ready to exit the program by about March or April. At that time, the person(s) overseeing this program may determine whether or not additional students should be added to take their places, but the number of students in each group should still not exceed four.

Once children begin showing improvement, teachers may be tempted to remove them from The Reading Club and replace them with students who are now performing at a lower level than Reading Club students. This is also a practice that should be avoided at all costs. The original students need the time to solidify and internalize the new skills and strategies they are learning. They also need time to develop confidence in themselves as literacy learners. Removing them from the support of the group prematurely most often results in a quick return to previous patterns of achievement. It is also difficult for the educational assistant to continually adapt to these changes in enrollment.

THE ROLE OF THE PRINCIPAL

The principal can play a pivotal role in the success of a program like The Reading Club. There are some key decisions a principal might make to signal the importance of the program. Several of these potential decisions are outlined below:

- Introduce the formation of The Reading Club program at a staff development session by having a presentation about the theoretical principles that undergird it and a demonstration of the session format.
- Designate a specific educational assistant(s) whose primary responsibility will be to work with Reading Club groups. Indicate that the assistant(s) cannot be removed from this responsibility to assist classroom teachers with other tasks except for emergencies or other rare, prearranged occasions.
- Indicate that students must be released for all assigned Reading Club sessions. Determine what special and rare occasions students may be released from sessions, e.g., class field trips.
- Ensure that all groups meet for a minimum of five sessions per week and for a minimum of 30 minutes per session.
- Provide opportunities for educational assistants to share student progress with classroom teachers.
- Provide quiet and well-lighted spaces for educational assistants to meet with their Reading Club groups. Ensure that there is ample space and privacy for the group to function effectively.
- Ensure that necessary materials are made available to facilitate the work of the groups and that there is a secure place for storage of materials.
- Provide release time for educational assistants to attend inservice sessions several times per semester.
- Ensure that educational assistants are allotted time to prepare student materials for the week.

SCHEDULING READING CLUB SESSIONS

Once the students have been selected and tested, the work of scheduling Reading Club sessions is ready to begin. There are a number of different configurations that schools may opt to use in scheduling. Some schools assign one educational assistant to each grade level to be involved. In a bilingual setting, it would be crucial to select an educational assistant who has strong literacy skills in both languages.

Another option would be to assign a particular educational assistant to a specific language. In these cases, the educational assistant would generally work with more than one grade level. In both scenarios it will be necessary to determine when students are to be involved in Reading Club sessions. Teachers may prefer to minimize the number of times students are removed from the work of the classroom. However, occasionally there will be a student whose work is significantly behind that of the rest of the Reading Club group. In these cases, a decision must be made about whether or not it is advisable for the student to join a group one grade level below his/her current grade level. This decision may also depend on how experienced the educational assistant is in meeting the needs of a diverse group. Placing students one grade level lower than their chronological age should only be done in extreme cases, as it may cause emotional stress for the students. If possible, individual sessions may be scheduled for students whose work is significantly lower than that of the other Reading Club students.

It will be important to establish guidelines for when Reading Club sessions take place within the context of the school curriculum as a whole. The principals featured in this guide have concluded that sessions are not to be scheduled during whole-class literacy instruction time in the classroom. They recognize the importance of ensuring that student learning not become fragmented due to participation in an outside group. They also wish to help students maintain a sense of membership in the collective literacy work of the classroom. Instead sessions were scheduled following the completion of whole-group instruction, when the class divides into smaller work groups. In this way one of the small groups could be a Reading Club session.

Both of the aforementioned principals administer bilingual schools. In this capacity, they also insist that Reading Club sessions not meet outside of scheduled English-as-a-Second Language (ESL) and/or Spanish-as-a-Second Language (SSL) sessions. Since the goals of the schools include literacy development in two languages, it is critical that students not be deprived of second-language instruction.

The consistency of these sessions is also of critical importance. As has been mentioned previously, erratic attendance (for whatever reason) usually derails potential progress in The Reading Club. We have found that the optimal situation consists of groups that meet for 45 minutes, four times per week. Reading Club sessions that meet for 30 minutes per day, five days per week also seem to be effective.

2

THE READING CLUB SESSIONS

All of the students who participate in The Reading Club have experienced difficulty in learning to read. Many of them have suffered lowered self-esteem as a result and do not see themselves as successful and competent learners. Therefore, it is of critical importance that Reading Club sessions be established in a very positive and supportive environment. It is also critical that groups be kept to four or fewer students, so that students in the greatest need of support receive the individualized attention they require.

Similar to Marie Clay's Reading Recovery Model (1985), each Reading Club session consists of four components: (1) introducing and reading a new book, (2) word works, (3) rereading previously read books, and (4) shared/independent writing. Each of these components is outlined below.

INTRODUCING AND READING A NEW BOOK

The first activity of each session centers on exploring and practicing a new book. The book remains a *new book* until all children in the group can read it with 100% accuracy, comprehend the plot, and exhibit confidence in reading it. The goals of this component of the lesson are to (1) help students focus on getting meaning from text, (2) teach and apply reading strategies, and (3) guide students in developing confidence in themselves as readers.

On the first day with a new book, the educational assistant introduces the title of the book and asks the children to predict what the story will be about. Students are guided to use the title and cover illustration to make predictions. With additional practice, educational assistants should guide students to use more and more details from the title and cover in making their predictions. Since making predictions is an important reading strategy, students should occasionally be given time to reflect on how well they use clues to make their predictions.

The educational assistant then leads the children in paging through the book to further reinforce what the story might be about and determine whether or not their initial predictions were valid. Initial reading of the book should focus on reading for comprehension and enjoyment. Early in the year, educational assistants working with first-grade students during the initial reading of the new book may wish to use echo reading, where the teacher reads a line of print and students echo or repeat the same line. It is important to stop at crucial points to highlight how picture and context clues aid comprehension and to discuss what is happening in the book. After the book has been enjoyed and discussed, the educational assistant and the children should reread the story together to solidify the content for the children.

We have found that many emergent readers in The Reading Club do not yet understand that print carries the meaning in reading. Therefore, we have beginning participants point to words as they are *reading* to help them begin to focus on print. Initially, there is often not a very close voice-to-print match in their reading, but this begins to improve with additional reading practice and through experiences in phonics (gained in the Word Works component of the session). Initially, students memorize the books, especially when patterned books are used, but with daily practice they begin to develop a sight-word vocabulary and acquire additional literacy skills and strategies.

On subsequent days, the educational assistant and the students should begin each lesson by reading the book together, making certain that students are sliding their fingers along the text and using picture clues where appropriate. When the students are able to read the book easily as a group, pairs or individuals can be asked to read the book to the rest of the group. Students should be supported as needed in their reading and never left to struggle individually in front of the group, as this may perpetuate their negative impressions of themselves as readers. If one or two students are experiencing difficulty reading the book individually, the educational assistant may wish to read along with them until they can read the book on their own.

Once the students can all read the book with 100% accuracy, it is time for the book to become a *reread* book, and a new book is selected for the next session. First-graders may require a full week or more to master their new book. Second-graders generally can move a bit more quickly. It is important to select books that are at the instructional level of the students, e.g., just slightly above the level of the students. In this way, they will quickly become successful with the material and develop a more positive attitude toward reading because they are not struggling to keep up. However, as soon as a particular level of books seems easy for the students, they should be given material that is slightly more difficult. Often, these students are one or more grade levels behind their peers. To reach grade-level expectations they must make more than one year of progress in an academic year. This process involves an intricate balance between moving the children along as quickly as possible and not exceeding their instructional level.

The new-book portion of the session is also the time to introduce and reinforce reading strategies. Educational assistants will have opportunities during inservice sessions to learn about these strategies and how to teach them. (See chapter 4 for more information about inservice sessions.) The first strategy generally deals with using picture cues to aid in getting meaning from print. Prediction, use of context clues, rereading, prior knowledge, and use of grapho-phonic cues are additional strategies that can be taught during the early stages of The Reading Club.

When students are reading and it is obvious that they have used a strategy to support learning, this should be pointed out to the group. "Did you notice how Juan made the /b/ sound and then looked at the picture to figure out the word 'bus'?" At other times the children can be asked to describe how they figured out a particular word or phrase. In this way students reach a metacognitive level of understanding about strategies, i.e., they are able to actively identify strategies and elaborate on how they used them to get meaning from print.

It is important to start slowly and make certain that students can use a particular strategy very effectively before beginning to teach a new strategy. It is also important to select reading material that lends itself well to the strategy being taught and practiced. For example, if students are being taught to predict with evidence, the plot of the story must include clues that could lead students to accurate predictions about what will happen in the text. If use of picture clues is the main focus, there should be very clear links between the pictures and the print on the page.

We have found that use of very brief pattern or predictable books works very well for emergent readers in The Reading Club. In these books, there is a limited set of vocabulary words and a great deal of repetition. The patterned nature of the story enables students to experience early success with a minimum of effort. However, it is also clear that eight-page books that merely provide one or two words per page are fine for a first book but do little to advance actual reading skills or understanding of story. The main benefit of these books is to draw student attention to use of picture cues and to encourage students to track print with their fingers.

If the pace appears too fast and the children are becoming frustrated, it may be necessary to slow the rate at which new material is added. The same is also true of the reread books that cannot be read easily and accurately by the children. This will mean that they were not ready to read these books independently and they should be returned to the new-book stage of the session. Occasionally, two or three of the students may reach this goal much more quickly than the other student(s). In these cases, the educational assistant, in consultation with the classroom teacher, must decide whether to rearrange the group configurations or to work separately with the child/children having difficulty.

WORD WORKS

During this portion of the Reading Club session, students are given the opportunity to explore how sounds and letters combine in word formation. This process is very closely aligned with the work of Marie Clay (1985), Patricia Cunningham (1995), and Fountas and Pinnell (1996) with Making Words in English. In Spanish, students use syllables as a base for studying new words.

Each child is given a set of letter cards for this exercise. The educational assistant works from a prepared list of the letters, sounds, words, and word parts that are to be practiced for the day. The same list is used until the children can readily identify and form the words and syllables without assistance.

The goal in these activities is not only to have students gain facility in identifying letters of the alphabet and the sounds represented by various combinations of letters but also to develop a broad repertoire of word analysis strategies. For example, students learn to recognize onset and rime patterns (formerly known as "word families"), e.g., *at, hat, sat, rat;* or look for words within words, "*and*" within the word "*sandy,*" for example. As students progress in their reading ability, they will have a greater range of strategies to use than just sounding words out letter by letter, especially since the English language has so many exceptions.

One of the characteristics of good emergent readers is that they read fluently (and with solid comprehension). When the reading behaviors of good readers are studied (Routman, 2000), it is clear that they do not sound out unfamiliar words on a letter-by-letter basis. They look for clues to help them decipher the word as quickly as possible so they can continue reading and processing the passage. For example, if a student was reading the sentence, "Taylor got a *brand*-new bike," and was stuck on the word *brand*, he might quickly see the word "and" within "brand," remember that Brianna's name starts with the /br/ sound and realize that "brand" makes sense in the sentence. All of this is processed in a split second and the child continues reading.

When children are first learning to read, the process is not very automatic. When they spend too much energy figuring out individual words, they lose sight of what they were reading about. There is a limited amount of information that can be held in short-term memory. Readers need to use most of that space to think about the author's message. Therefore, the goal is to have children develop large sight-word vocabularies and a well-developed set of word-recognition strategies so the bulk of their efforts can be focused on meaning and not on decoding.

The Word Works component is designed to accomplish both of these objectives. As students practice forming words and exploring patterns, they add words to their sight vocabularies, i.e., words they recognize automatically. Secondly, they expand their ability to use a broader range of strategies for figuring out words they do not instantly recognize. As mentioned previously, these strategies include sound/letter patterns, words within words, syllables, and links to other known words and patterns.

The process used in Word Works is different in English and in Spanish. A sample lesson for each language is outlined below.

In English the students might be given the letters for the word "plant" in random order. This version of wordplay was developed by Clay (1985) and Cunningham (1995) and enables the children to make several smaller words using the letters from the word of the day. The final word formation requires the students to use all of the letters to make a word; in this case, "plant."

The letter cards (which are available commercially) should have the lowercase letter on one side and the uppercase letter on the reverse side. The consonants are often on white card stock and the vowels on yellow card stock. Ask the children to separate the vowels from the consonants and identify each of the letters. This also reinforces letter recognition for students who do not yet know all of their letters. Below is a sample Word Works lesson in English:

1. What two letters would give you the word *an*? (Students place the two letters on the table in front of themselves.)
   - Point to each letter and spell the word. ("*a-n* spells *an*.")
   - What word does this give us? (Say "*an*.")
   - How many syllables does the word *an* have? (Children clap the word and say "one.")
2. What letter could you put in front of *an* to make the word *tan*? "Yes, *t*."
   - Point to each letter and spell the word *tan*. ("*t-a-n* spells *tan*.")
   - How many syllables does the word *tan* have?
3. Put the *t* back. What letter could you add to *an* to make the word *pan*?
   - Point to each letter and spell the word *pan*. ("*p-a-n* spells *pan*.")
   - How many syllables does the word *pan* have?
   - Now put all of the letters back.
4. What two letters would give you the /ap/ sound? (Students place the two letters in front of themselves.)

- Point to each letter and spell the sound. (*"a-p* spells *ap."*)
- What letter could you put in front of *ap* to make the word *lap?*
- Point to each letter and spell the word *lap.* (*"l-a-p* spells *lap."*)
- How many syllables does the word *lap* have? (Children clap the word and say "one.")

5. Put the *l* back. Now make the word *tap.* What letter did you put at the beginning of the word?
   - Point to each letter and spell the word *tap.* (*"t-a-p* spells *tap."*)
   - How many syllables does the word *tap* have?

6. Put the *t* back. Now make the word *nap.* What letter did you put at the beginning of the word?
   - Point to each letter and spell the word *nap.* (*"n-a-p* spells *nap."*)
   - How many syllables does the word *nap* have?
   - Now put all of the letters back.

7. Put out the letters *a, n.* What does that spell? (*"a-n* spells *an."*)
   - Put a *t* at the end of the word. What does that spell? (*"a-n-t* spells *ant."*)
   - Now put a *p* in front of *ant.* What does that spell?
   - Use all of the letters to make a new word.
   - What word did you make? Point to each letter and spell the word. (*"p-l-a-n-t* spells *plant."*)

This type of activity allows children to experiment with the ways in which words are put together. For many students it becomes a way to begin to unlock the mysteries of words. They begin to recognize that there are patterns and that they can often use what they already know to figure out new words. Students who are experiencing reading difficulties often approach each reading experience as if everything is new. The word-recognition strategies they learn in this portion of the lesson help them approach new words with greater skill and confidence.

Below is a sample Word Works lesson in Spanish. In Spanish, Word Works centers on the formation of syllables for emergent readers. If the new letter of the session is *m,* for example, the lesson would focus on the syllables *ma, me, mi, mo, mu,* and combinations of those syllables to form words.

In this sense, the Spanish Word Works section suggests the notion of a "controlled vocabulary," i.e., only words that can be formed with previously introduced letters and syllables are used in making new words. The same letter cards used in Word Works in English may be used for Spanish, with the addition of the letters *ñ* and *ll* and accented vowel cards.

1. Pongan las vocales en orden. ¿Cuáles son? (<<*a-e-i-o-u*>>.)
   - ¿Qué consonante tenemos hoy? (<<*m*>>.)
   - Forman el sonido /*ma*/ usando dos letras.
   - Usan el dedo para indicar las letras y deletrean *ma*. (<<*m-a* dice *ma*>>.)
2. Guardan la letra *a* y forman el sonido /*mo*/ con dos letras. ¿Qué dice? (<<*mo*>>.)
   - Usan el dedo para indicar las letras y deletrean. (<<*m-o* dice *mo*>>.)
3. Guardan la letra *o* y forman el sonido /*me*/ con dos letras. ¿Qué dice? (<<*me*>>.)
   - Usan el dedo para indicar las letras y deletrean. (<<*m-e* dice *me.*>>)
   - Es una palabra también, ¿no?
4. Guardan la letra *e* y forman el sonido /*mu*/ con dos letras. ¿Qué dice? (<<*mu*>>.)
   - Usan el dedo para indicar las letras y deletrean. (<<*m-u* dice *mu*>>.)
5. Guardan la letra *u* y forman el sonido /*mi*/ con dos letras. ¿Qué dice? (<<*mi*>>.)
   - Usan el dedo para indicar las letras y deletrean. (<<*m-i* dice *mi*>>.)
   - Es una palabra también, ¿no?
6. Ahora vamos a formar una palabra con tres letras, *amo*. ¿Qué dice? (<<*amo*>>.)
   - Usan el dedo para indicar las letras y deletrean *amo*. (<<*a-m-o* dice *amo*>>.)
   - ¿Cuántas sílabas hay en la palabra *amo*?
   - (Aplauden: <<*dos*>>.) Dividen la palabra en dos partes: *a/mo*.
   - Guardan la letra *o*.
   - ¿Qué letra pueden poner para formar la palabra *ama*?
   - Usan el dedo y deletrean *ama*. (<<*a-m-a* dice *ama*>>.)
7. Ahora vamos a formar una palabra con cuatro letras, "*mamá*." ¿Qué dice? (<<*mamá*>>.)

- Usan el dedo para indicar las letras y deletrean "*mamá.*" (*<<m-a-m-á* dice *mamá>>.*)
- ¿Cuántas sílabas hay en la palabra *mamá*?
- (Aplauden: *<<dos>>.*) Dividen la palabra en dos partes: *ma/má.*

For the second lesson, *p* might be chosen as the new consonant. The students would begin by forming the syllables: *pa, pe, pi, po, pu.* New words would then be formed using the syllables from sessions one and two, such as; *papá, pipa*, and *mapa.*

The Word Works exercises can be varied to give students greater flexibility. Sometimes we may tell them how many letters are needed to form a certain word. "Use three letters to make the word 'wet.'" Or the educational assistant may also occasionally use the letters to make words already studied for the children to identify.

Some children may be able to select the correct letters (or some of them) for the words, but they may not know whether to start spelling the word moving to the left or to the right. The educational assistant should show them that they always start on the left and work to the right. Putting a dot on the table with an arrow pointing to the right might be helpful. Children would then know to start at the dot and work to the right. If a child has all the correct letters but they are not in the correct order, the educational assistant might tell the child, "You have all the right letters but they are mixed up," and say the word slowly. For example; if the child put out the letters *ast* for the word *sat*: "Ssssaaatttt. What sound do we hear at the beginning of this word?" "Yes, /s/. What letter gives us the /s/ sound?" "Very good, *s.*"

Initially some students may have little or no idea about what they are expected to do in these exercises. They may not know all of their letters, and they may not realize that there are sounds associated with letters. For this reason, these activities should be conducted in a very non-threatening and supportive manner. The children should be allowed to look at the work of their classmates to form their own responses. Asking children to form a word when they have no clue about how to spell the word, or even how individual letters sound, puts them in an awkward situation. Most will begin to catch on after a few sessions.

The educational assistant should assist individual students who are having difficulty but guide them to be as independent as possible. For example, in forming the word *an,* let's say the student put down the *a* but was not certain of the second letter. Rather than simply giving the student the next letter, the assistant could ask, "What sound makes the /n/ sound at the end of *an*?," repeating the sound two or three times so the child can clearly hear it. If the child still does not know the letter associated with the sounds, the assistant can *then* point to the letter and let the child put it in place to form the word.

It is very important that the children have the opportunity to physically manipulate the letter cards in making the words and join in on spelling and pointing to the words. Research has shown (Jensen, 1998a, 1998b) that children learn more fully and retain more of what they learn when they use as many of the senses as possible in the learning activities. J. W. Riley provides each child with a small plastic tub containing the magnetic letters to be used in the day's lesson. The letters are three-dimensional and allow children to actually feel and see the shape of the letters. Another component of this philosophy involves having the children point to each letter when spelling a word (or pointing to each word while reading). Eventually children will not need to do this, but initially it helps them focus on individual letters and aids in memory.

Repetition is a key element in Word Works. Although children may not recognize letters and sounds the first time that they are introduced, after three to four days of practice they generally begin to work independently. It is very important to make certain that children know the first set of words/word parts very well before moving on to subsequent sets of words. What has happened to many of these children is that they did not understand the concepts when they were studied in the classroom, but because most of the other children in the classroom did understand them, the teacher moved on to more challenging work. The result was that these children fell further and further behind their classmates because they did not have a firm base on which to scaffold new learning. Some have come to believe that they cannot keep up, so they do not pay close attention to what they are being asked to do. If this is the case, it may take some time for them to build up their level of confidence. The Reading Club is structured to enable students to be successful from the beginning.

The initial screening will provide a good indication of which letters of the alphabet the children do and do not know. Students can be given a set of cards containing the letters they do not yet know. These could be punched and placed on a ring. Each day students review these letter cards at the end of the session (or when first arriving) for two or three minutes. This could be done independently, in pairs, or with the educational assistant. For students who know very few letters, it would be best to only focus on two or three letters at a time, adding additional letters when the first ones have been learned.

Students are guided through a series of word/letter patterns in the Word Works section, but it is not an end in itself. Whenever words, rhyming words, or other patterns that have been studied are also represented in the day's reading, this should be pointed out. We can highlight the links that we notice between Word Works and actual reading passages, but we can also frequently ask the students, "What did you notice in this story?" (or "with these words?") We want children to become good observers about their reading. For example, a child might say, "We made the word *pan* this morning, so I figured out that the boy's name is *Dan* because it has the /an/ sound." The object of Word Works is to give children strategies that make them better readers, not just better decoders. (See appendix E for suggested Word Works materials in English and in Spanish.)

It is best to start with the letter cards or magnetic letters that children can physically manipulate and use them until the children begin to work quite quickly with new word lists. At this point, the letter cards can be replaced with Word Works notebooks. Students can be told how many letters are in the new word. They open their notebooks to the Word Works section and draw that number of dashes on the line, while the educational assistant does the same on the board or a large sheet of paper. The children write the words one by one and divide them into syllables. After each word is completed, the educational assistant writes it on the board, or an individual student volunteers to write the word. The group spells the word together and each child corrects his/her own work.

Educational assistants will need time to prepare the letter cards or bins of magnetic letters for each group. If preparation time is not allotted, educational assistants must find a quick and efficient way to distribute needed materials. Providing each student with a large assortment of letters is not recommended because valuable class time will be lost with children searching for letters. Both of the schools featured in this book have purchased boxes from hardware stores that have multiple small drawers for the storage of small objects. They put all of the *a* cards in the first drawer, *b* cards in the second, etc. This makes for quick access to letters, but it is still better use of class time if this is completed before the children arrive. Other educational assistants have put together four sets of word cards (one for each child) and put them in an envelope labeled with the lesson number. In this way, the materials are ready when needed and can be stored for use with subsequent groups.

REREADING

One of the simplest yet most critical aspects of Reading Club sessions is the rereading of previously read books. It serves both to reinforce reading skills and strategies that have already been studied and to enhance the self-esteem of the students as competent readers. Because the books are easily reread by the children, they begin to feel a level of proficiency as readers.

Frequently, emergent readers initially memorize simple books rather than actually reading them. This is especially true of pattern books. If children are provided opportunities to reread and encouraged to point to individual words as they read, they come to recognize more and more words. In addition to increasing their sight-word vocabularies, rereading books helps them improve their understanding of the organization of narrative and expository text. This is especially critical if they have not been read to a great deal outside of school. With practice, they come to expect that stories will involve characters who are in the process of trying to solve a problem or that texts contain information about a particular topic.

Once a book can be read with 100% accuracy by the children in the group during the *new-book* phase, it becomes eligible for designation as a *reread book*. Obviously, when the program first starts, there will be no books designated as reread books, so the first book can be reread during this part of the session. All of the books that can be read independently with 100% accuracy are placed in the center of the table during the *reread session*. Students read each of these books independently or in pairs.

It is suggested that the children maintain a list of books that they can read (see appendix F). This also serves as a great reinforcement, as they see the growing list of books that they can successfully read. As the number of books grows to several books (more than seven or eight), educational assistants may wish to remove the first books. At this point, students may be tiring of these initial stories. As students progress to reading longer and longer texts, the rereading session may be scaled back but should not be completely eliminated, as it provides opportunities for students to solidify reading skills and strategies, as mentioned previously. As students begin reading beginning novels or longer picture books, they may be asked to reread certain passages for specific purposes. For example, students can be asked to reread favorite parts, passages that led them to make certain predictions, passages used as evidence to support inferences, etc.

Occasional use of a self-assessment checklist is recommended to provide opportunities for students to reflect on their independent reading. Categories might include use of specific strategies, fluency, and comprehension. During brief one-on-one conferences, the educational assistant may ask students to demonstrate one or more of these categories. (See appendix F for examples of student self-assessment forms.)

SHARED/INDEPENDENT WRITING

The final component of The Reading Club focuses on engaging students in independent and shared writing. It is important to ensure that this element is not ignored. Reading and writing are very closely linked. Children generally enhance their understanding of reading through writing, and they improve their writing through reading.

The process for writing should always contain two components: (1) students write and (2) students share what they have written. Since children will finish their writing at different times, a routine could be established whereby each child reads his/her writing to the educational assistant when she/he finishes. One or two children could share with the whole group or with a partner each day, also.

Shared writing involves the group brainstorming and writing a piece together. While the topic for writing could be preselected in shared writing, there should be *many* opportunities for students to select their topics and organize their own writing. Initially, the writing sessions may involve writing patterned stories (see below) based on predictable books read in the new-book section. As the name implies, during independent writing children write independently on self-selected topics. Children may select a new topic each day or continue with a single topic for several days.

There are various stages of writing, and children must pass through each stage to get to the next. Children need many opportunities to practice and examine their writing at each stage. It is important that educational assistants be familiar with the stages of writing that children progress through. For a discussion of the stages of writing and other aspects of teaching writing, see chapter 4, *Stages of Reading and Writing*.

Student writing should be reviewed to determine the stage at which each child is writing. Knowing this and what to look for at each stage of writing will provide the educational assistant with ideas about what to expect next from student writing.

One of the educational assistants at Hayes developed a very useful set of writing rules for his second-grade Club de Lectura groups that helped students improve their writing a great deal. He noted common errors that students were making and put them on a list of writing rules. The list included the following rules:

- Begin each sentence with a capital letter.
- End each sentence with a period, question mark, or exclamation point.
- Do not repeat. Start each sentence differently.
- Write only one *and* for each sentence.

The educational assistants then developed a rubric from the writing rules and taught children to self-assess their own writing (see chapter 3). They required students to revise their writing when some of the rules were not followed. Within a few weeks students were following the writing rules without prompting. Too often children who are struggling are not held to these expectations and their writing continues without improvement in mechanics. The use of this simple set of writing rules proved to us that with consistent use, the children quite easily developed these skills.

A writing journal might be prepared for students' daily writing. Sometimes children have a difficult time coming up with a topic to write about. Often this means that the children are unsure about their writing; therefore, they are hesitant to begin. Having brief discussions about possible writing topics will often generate ideas—and enthusiasm. Sharing finished pieces also allows students to model their work for one another. About once a month have students look back at earlier writing to note progress.

The Hayes Two-Way Bilingual School was using the Power Writing technique (Sparks, 1982) as a schoolwide writing approach. The principal suggested that this technique be applied to El Club de Lectura both as a way to improve writing and as an opportunity to link the work of El Club de Lectura to the school initiative. In Power Writing, the child generates a topic and three supporting details as a prewriting activity. The ideas can be delineated on a graphic organizer. An umbrella organization containing the main topic and placing the subordinate ideas follows. If the main topic is "Fun at the park," for example, this topic would appear in the umbrella, and the subtopic that the children select—"Play on the swings," "Swim at the pool," "Climb trees"—appears below. During the actual writing time, the children write an introductory sentence that mentions the topic and names the supporting details. This is followed by a sentence or paragraph (depending on the age and stage of writing of the group) on each of the supporting details.

Another way to approach writing in The Reading Club is to outline a progression of writing activities for the children to engage in during the semester. Each activity is organized to require more writing and greater independence than the previous activities. A number of alternative writing suggestions are outlined below.

Pattern Books: Innovation on a Text

This is a very basic initial writing activity. Children read a pattern book and then use the pattern of the book to write their own story, substituting key words with their own ideas. A sample is shown in table 2.1.

Table 2.1. Sample Substitution Table for a Pattern Book

Original Text	Substitutions
"Lunch"	"Lunch with Grandma"
Today I went shopping with *my mother*.	grandma
We bought some *bread*.	buns
We bought some *peanut butter*.	hot dogs
We bought some *jelly*.	chips
We bought some *milk*.	juice
We bought some *apples*.	grapes
Then we went *home* and made a nice lunch.	to grandma's house

During the new book portion of the class, the group would read and practice the story "Lunch." After the children were quite confident in reading the story, the educational assistant would begin working on writing the new version of the text (also referred to as an innovation on a text). Note that in table 2.1, key words have been italicized. These words will change, but the rest of the pattern will remain the same. Children must identify who they wish to go shopping with and what they will make for lunch. Write the new version of the story, "Lunch with Grandma," on a large sheet of paper (figure 2.1) and have the children help with spelling as you write. Reread the story together two or three times.

Prepare several four-page booklets for use in these initial patterned or predictable stories. Give each child a booklet and have the students copy one sentence per page into the booklets, encouraging them to read as they write. Children may illustrate the booklet when they finish, but take care not to spend a lot of time on the artwork. Review the new version of the story each day at the beginning of the writing session. Have children read the booklet to you when they finish or during the reread section of the lesson.

Once the children understand the process of making a new version of a story, let them do the innovations independently. It is critical that the students not become dependent on the educational assistant for generating writing ideas. Some students will begin to enjoy writing and will be anxious to take off on their own. Others will need extra coaching to work more independently. It may take a little time and practice to encourage students to accept more independence in their writing, so some rocky beginnings should be anticipated.

Today I went shopping with my grandma.
We bought some buns.
We bought some hot dogs.
We bought some chips.
We bought some juice.
We bought some grapes.
Then we went to grandma's house and made a nice lunch.

Figure 2.1. "Lunch with Grandma," an innovation of the text "Lunch."

Think of a story idea.
Make a pattern.
Make a list of ideas to fit the pattern.
Make an ending.

Figure 2.2. Guidelines for Organizing Pattern Book Ideas.

Pattern Books: Independent Patterns

At this point children begin making their own pattern books. It may be a good idea to outline one or two as a group first, to make certain that the children understand the process. Begin by having them review the patterns in books they've already read. Have them note that a topic is introduced for the book, followed by a repeating pattern of events. They should also notice that the ending changes the pattern and allows the story to end. Figure 2.2 provides a guideline for helping students organize their ideas for a pattern book. Figure 2.3 provides a prewriting sample for use in pattern-book planning. Other topic ideas for stories might include:

- People who work at my school
- Places I go with my family
- Going grocery shopping (for lunch, breakfast, etc.)
- Baby animals
- What children like to do

Have students keep their story booklets in their folders for rereading and as a record of how much writing they have actually completed. If students wish to share their work with their families, allow them to take

Story idea: Things I do at school
Pattern: I can _____ at school.
List of ideas for pattern: color, sing, play, read, work
Ending: I have fun at school all day long.

Figure 2.3. Prewriting Sample for Planning a Pattern Book.

home one booklet at a time and return it to the folder the next day. The more they share their reading and writing, the more practice they are getting. When students take home work that they can read very fluently, parents feel their children are making good progress and children experience success in sharing with their parents.

Letter Writing: Independent Writing

A next writing activity might revolve around letter writing. This would be another step in building independence in writing, as most children could generate the content completely on their own.

It would be helpful to share some well-written letters from children and to review the format for letter writing with the children. Using a very simple format (salutation, body, closing) will be sufficient for most students. Doing a shared writing of a letter or two (perhaps to the classroom teacher, principal, etc.) could serve as a good transitional activity in preparation for independent letter writing.

A variety of stationery, cards, and postcards can be kept on hand for these activities. Reading Club or school stationery could even be designed for use in these letter writing activities. If children wish to actually send some of the letters, it would be important to have them edited first. Make a copy for the child's writing folder and send the original off to the recipient.

Information Books and Poems: Mapping

In this writing format, children select a topic they know a lot about and make an informational booklet. This is a great way to have children begin mapping and classifying information before writing.

A first step is to have students brainstorm a list of topics they know a lot about. For example, a list might include the following ideas: dogs, friends, family, toys, football teams, and fun places to go. The writer would need to review the list and select the topic she/he liked the most and knew the most about. Other topics could be reserved for later booklets.

If the topic selected is "dogs," for instance, the group would then create a map or web of all the things they could write about relating to dogs (see figure 2.4). Next have the children talk abut what they want to write about first, second, etc. After the students have written two or three informational booklets, they could begin to classify the information on

Dogs:
- are different sizes
- are different breeds

They like to:
- bark
- run
- fetch sticks
- lick your face

They need to be taken care of:
- must be fed
- must be taken for a walk
- must be played with

They can be helpful:
- round up cattle
- be a seeing-eye dog
- be a fire dog

Some are dangerous.

Figure 2.4. Brainstorming "Map" for Writing about Dogs.

Dogs

1. There are many different kinds of dogs:
   different sizes
   different breeds
2. We must take care of our dogs:
   feed them
   take them for a walk
3. Dogs can be lots of fun:
   run and bark
   play with you
   fetch sticks
   lick your face
4. Some dogs work for a living:
   seeing-eye dogs
   fire dogs
   cattle dogs

Figure 2.5. Sample Organization for Writing about Dogs.

their webs and organize their writing ideas into categories (or even chapters). See figure 2.5 for a sample of organizing writing ideas.

Another option might be to have students create poems about their topics. One suggestion would be to share *The Important Book* (1949) by Margaret Wise Brown and examine the pattern she uses in describing objects. Each poem begins with "The important thing about a _____ is that it is _____" and ends with "But the important thing about a _____ is that it is_____." In the body of the poem there is a listing of other important points about the object. See figure 2.6 for a sample poem from *The Important Book* (pp. 11–12).

Students will need to determine what is most important about their topic and other points that should also be included. For example, using the "dog" map (figure 2.4), an "important" poem might look like the one in figure 2.7. Each line can become a page in their booklets.

Book Reviews; Opinions with Evidence

As children read various books, it is important for them to think about whether or not they enjoyed them. Some students learn to read well but have not come to realize that reading should have an impact on them. Good readers can evaluate books according to whether or not they enjoyed them or learned something from them. They can identify favorite authors and types or genres of books (fairy tales, informational books, poetry, adventure books, etc.).

The important thing about an apple is that it is round.
It is red,
You bite it,
And it is white inside,
And the juice splashes in your face,
And it tastes like an apple,
And it falls off a tree.
But the important thing about an apple is that it is round.

Figure 2.6.   Poem from *The Important Book* by Margaret Wise Brown.

The most important thing about dogs is that they lick your face.
They bark,
And wag their tails,
And sometimes can even bite.
They like to run,
And fetch sticks,
And be petted.
They will guard your house at night.
But the important thing about dogs is that they lick your face.

Figure 2.7. "Important" Poem about Dogs.

A first step in helping children think about the books they've read is to ask them to select their favorite book from the reread books. Use a book that several of the children have enjoyed and have the group brainstorm what they liked about the book. Together, they can write a review of the book as a shared writing experience.

The reviews can be put on large index cards and placed in a box for children to share with one another. Children may also write reviews about books they did not like. The important thing is for children to form opinions about books and be able to provide evidence to support their opinions. See table 2.2 for a sample book review.

Fairy Tales: Character, Setting, and Plot

Brainstorm who the characters usually are in fairy tales, where the story usually takes place, and what usually happens in a fairy tale. See

Table 2.2. Sample Book Review

Organizer	Book Review
Name of book: *Lunch*	Lunch
What I liked about this book	You will like this book.
Funny pictures	The pictures are very funny.
Pattern book	It is easy to read because it is a pattern book.
Make lunch	The girl gets to eat lunch with her mom.

table 2.3 for a sample characteristics chart. Special language used in fairy tales may also be included.

Students could create a web for their story and organize the plot before beginning to write. By this point in their writing, students should be able to write a draft, edit and revise it, and then write a final copy. The draft could be written in their journals and the final copy in a booklet or on special paper.

Adventure Stories (Suspense) and Mysteries (Clues)

The same process used with fairy tales could be used in planning for and writing adventure stories and mysteries. It would be most effective if students had already read books in these genres before attempting to write their own stories to ensure that they have a good sense of how these stories are structured. In writing adventure stories, students could focus on what creates suspense. In writing mysteries, they might determine what the mystery is and how it will be solved and then create clues that would lead to solving the mystery.

These are suggestions for enhancing writing activities in The Reading Club. Activities should be selected that are easy and enjoyable for the children, but that hold a bit of challenge for them. The activities suggested here are organized from simplest to most complex. Children in first grade may not get beyond the first three or four activities. Most of these activities will take more than a single session to complete. The writing portion of the session may include a mix of journal writing and the activities suggested above. If children are writing vigorously every

Table 2.3.　Sample Characteristics Chart (Fairy Tales)

Characters	Setting	Plot	Special Language
Royals	castle	defeat a bad person	Once upon a time
Queen	forest	trick someone	happily ever after
King	village	prince finds a wife	special potion
Prince	farm		
Princess			
Fairy godmother			
Animals that talk			
Bad person/animal			

day, let them continue. If they are not accomplishing much during each session, the educational assistant will need to guide them along, helping them set goals for what should be completed each day. Art-work is an important component of student writing but should not overshadow writing time. Students who wish to include more elaborate art work might be allowed to complete it at home and bring it to school the next day.

3

ASSESSING STUDENT PROGRESS

Assessment is a critical component of The Reading Club. A variety of assessments are used to monitor student progress, guide instruction, and provide students with mechanisms to gauge their own growth.

Screening tests are given in fall, winter, and spring as samples of student literacy development. The screening tests consist of alphabet recognition, word lists, reading, miscue analysis and comprehension check, dictation, and a writing sample. The tests are administered individually to each of the students. Sample test materials in English and Spanish can be found in appendix D.

Educational assistants would need to be inserviced on the components and administration of the screening tests prior to administering them. It is recommended that someone experienced in testing work with the educational assistants until they feel confident enough to proceed on their own. Initial screening can take a long time to complete; therefore, if an additional person skilled in test administration is assigned to assist with this process, it can speed up this part of the schedule immensely.

It is important to make the children feel as relaxed as possible when they come into the testing area. Chatting with them briefly before beginning the screening test will help in this endeavor. Make certain the testing area is quiet and well lighted. At the beginning of the screening session, children should be told, "We want to see what you can do *on your own* in reading and writing, so I will not be able to help you. Do your best but don't worry if you make some mistakes."

The screening test is not timed, and students should be given ample time to respond. On the word lists, allow children to indicate if they cannot figure a word out and move on to the next item. In initial screening sessions in the fall, students may not be able to complete many of the activities. This becomes the baseline data to measure how much progress they make throughout the year. *Be certain to date all materials* so it will be possible to monitor student progress over time. Administration of each component of the screening test is outlined below.

ALPHABET RECOGNITION

Students are given a large-type alphabet sheet, and educational assistants mark student responses in identifying the letters on a recording sheet, circling any errors as the students read the letters. If an incorrect letter is given, the letter is circled as an error and the student response is written next to the letter. After the students have completed the alphabet recognition test, the assistants record unknown letters in the spaces provided. These become the letters for each child to study on a daily basis.

WORD LISTS

Educational assistants may wish to laminate a set of word lists for the children to use and record their responses on the individual recording sheets found in appendix D. In this second activity students begin reading a list of words at the PP (preprimer) level and continue reading until they fall into the frustration level. The independent, instructional, and frustration levels are indicated at the bottom of each word list. Although it is very tempting to help children decode the words, it is important to resist this temptation. The purpose of the screening is to determine what skills and strategies students can employ independently.

There are two columns next to each list of words labeled "Sight" and "Analysis." "Sight" words are words the child instantly recognizes. Put a check in the "Sight" column if the child reads the word without hesitation. "Analysis" refers to sounding the word out. Put a check in this column if the child sounded the word out letter by letter or syllable by syllable. Both types of responses are correct and should be counted in the "Number Correct" at the end of the list. If the student responds with a word other than the word indicated on the list, write this word next to the actual word and count it as an error.

READING FLUENCY AND COMPREHENSION

A set of leveled books may be set aside for use only for screening purposes, or a commercially prepared Informal Reading Inventory (IRI) may be used to assess reading fluency and comprehension.

If the school chooses to compile its own set of leveled books, one book will need to be selected from each level beginning with PP (preprimer) and proceeding to just beyond the highest grade level to be included in The Reading Club. For example, if students in first and second grades are to be involved, the reading material must go through at least level 3.1. These books should only be used for testing and not as reading materials during the sessions or in the classroom. The easiest way (though time-consuming initially) to prepare these materials is to record the books on data sheets as in figure 3.1. The child reads from the actual book and the educational assistant records his/her responses on the reading evaluation form.

As the child reads, the examiner marks a check above each word on the reading evaluation form that was read correctly and indicates any miscues the child made. (See inservice section on miscue analysis.) After reading, the student is asked to tell what the story was about. The examiner scores the child as a 1, 2, or 3 depending on the accuracy of the

| Name: _____ | Date: _____ |

| **Lunch** | **Meaning** | **Sound** | **Visual** |

Today I went shopping with my mother.
We bought some bread.
We bought some peanut butter.
We bought some jelly.
We bought some milk.
Then we went home and made a nice lunch.

Figure 3.1.   Sample Reading Evaluation Form.

The student was:

_____ able to accurately retell the story. (3 points)

_____ was able to accurately retell some of the story. (2 points)

_____ was unable to retell the story/inaccurately retold the story. (1 point)

Comprehension Score: _____

Analysis of reading (check all that apply)

Did the student:

_____ read the story accurately and fluently?

_____ look only at the pictures and make up the story?

_____ use pictures to help figure out the words?

_____ sound out words?

_____ not know what to do when he/she came to an unknown word?

_____ read the story accurately but very hesitantly and slowly?

Figure 3.2.   Reading Score Form and Reading Behavior Checklist.

retelling. (See figure 3.2. This figure also provides a checklist of reading behaviors that the examiner can look for.) A few well-designed questions about the story may replace the retelling as a measure of student comprehension of their reading.

The advantage of having a leveled set of books for screening is that children have an actual book in their hands. There are more pictures and less print per page than on IRIs, which makes the task seem less daunting to children.

In both the IRI and the leveled books, if a child reads the first book or story with few or no errors, proceed to the next book until the reading becomes too difficult or the child is unable to retell what she/he has read.

A number of IRIs are available commercially (Stieglitz, 2002; Leslie and Caldwell, 2001; Burns and Roe, 2002; Rhodes, 1993). The Flynt-Cooter (1998) is available in English and Spanish, which may be of interest to English–Spanish bilingual schools. The advantages of the IRIs are that all of the materials are part of a concise test book, including professionally leveled stories and corresponding comprehension questions. Reading passages may be laminated for use by the child, and the examiner can mark miscues on recording sheets.

In both situations, reading passages for several levels must be on hand to allow each child to read to his or her highest level. The educational assistants at Hayes and Riley make a set of all reading-passage levels for each child. Unused materials are stored for use in assembling the packets for the next screening sessions.

DICTATION

In this activity, the educational assistant reads a series of four sentences one at a time, and the child writes each on a sheet of paper. Each sentence has been designed to reveal student ability to use certain aspects of grammar, punctuation, and spelling.

This activity might be substituted by having the children write a list of all the words they are quite certain they can spell correctly.

WRITING

Ask children to write about a topic of their own choosing. Encourage them to write as much as they can about the topic, but do not offer assistance. If they cannot think of a topic, brainstorm with them to select a topic they'd enjoy writing about. If they ask for help in spelling words, remind them that we want to see how much they can do on their own and to spell each word as best they can. Each child's writing should be evaluated to determine at what level she/he is writing. (See chapter 4 for an overview of the stages of writing.)

Time must be set aside for educational assistants to prepare all of the screening materials for the children. Some schools prepare a file for each child and keep all of the assessment materials in this file. The files should be stored in a location that is secure but that the educational assistant can access easily. Also, preparing files of materials that need to be copied for the screening test will facilitate preparation of materials for subsequent testing sessions.

After all of the screening tests have been completed, they should be reviewed by the educational assistant, classroom teachers, and other school personnel involved in overseeing The Reading Club (principal, reading teacher, etc.). Students who score at or above grade level or significantly higher than other students identified for possible membership in The Reading Club should be reconsidered. Other students who are not officially identified as having special needs but who perhaps would score lower than the student(s) tested could also be tested and replace the child(ren) who scored higher on the screening.

Schools that offer literacy instruction in more than one language will have additional considerations to make in reviewing the screening information. Language dominance is an issue that should be considered in establishing a Reading Club in your school. In first grade, and often in second grade as well, students will make the most progress when learning to read and write in their dominant language. At higher grade levels, students who are reading at grade level in their dominant language but struggling in their second language may work in their second language in The Reading Club.

Occasionally, students enter the program who have begun literacy instruction in one language, based on parent preference and/or language dominance testing, but prefer their other language and use it more extensively. For example, if the child is considered Spanish-dominant but speaks in English whenever an opportunity presents itself, this might be an indication that the child is more comfortable in English, and that will need to be taken into account when determining the language of instruction.

The screening results should also be reviewed to determine areas of strength or weakness for each group. This will determine the level of materials to be used in the first work sessions. After the winter and spring testing sessions, the results should be evaluated to determine student progress. Care should be given to areas where students have made significant progress and areas where little or no progress has been made. In the areas where little or no progress has been made, changes should be made to the daily work sessions to improve these areas.

It is very valuable (and enjoyable) for students to examine their progress from one screening session to the next. Set aside time during a lesson to allow students to compare their earlier test results with their present level of accomplishment. They often become very excited to see their progress, and this translates to renewed effort and enthusiasm in the work sessions. This type of self-assessment allows children to begin taking more ownership of their learning.

Communication with the classroom teachers is very important but is often not very easy to accomplish. Having students share some of their work with the classroom teachers is a great avenue for maintaining connections between the teacher and The Reading Club. This could involve having the child read to the teacher from books practiced in the Reading Club sessions, sharing writing samples, etc. Often this enables the classroom teacher to build on the work of The Reading Club. In our experience, the students who made the most progress came from classes where the classroom teacher was most involved in the children's work in both venues. While it *is* important to maintain good communication with the classroom teachers, it is also important that teachers not send work from the classroom to be completed in the Reading Club session. This defeats the purpose of the program and reduces it to a resource center. Some teachers share materials from The Reading Club with parents during parent-teacher conferences as additional evidence of student progress. Educational assistants may be invited to join these conferences and further explain the children's work.

RUBRICS AND SELF-ASSESSMENT

In addition to the screening instruments, rubrics are used on a regular basis to help children self-assess their progress in reading and writing. As mentioned in the independent/shared writing section, one of the educational assistants from Hayes developed a list of writing rules that was later converted to a writing rubric (see appendix F).

For emergent literacy groups it might be easier to have students begin focusing only on capital letters and periods. Other writing rules could be added after the first ones are being followed consistently.

The writing rules become a self-assessment writing rubric when children are asked to critique and rate their writing. At first, children may not be very adept at judging their own work. However, with guidance and practice they will learn what to look for. When a student completes a rubric on his/her writing she/he should review it with the educational assistant. If there are errors on points that have already been emphasized, the educational assistant may wish to have the student correct them in the writing. For beginning readers, the educational assistant may read the rules with the students and review them orally.

A focus on the content of the writing has been added to the writing rubric to ensure that students focus on both mechanics *and* content of their writing in carrying out their self-assessment (see appendix F).

Teaching students to use strategies to improve their reading and writing is a major focus in The Reading Club. Strategy development is discussed more fully in chapter 5, but a process for assessing reading is presented here. Students should be taught the strategies one by one, followed by ample opportunities to practice them. Occasionally, they should be asked to reflect on their reading and their use of strategies. Appendix F contains Spanish and English versions of a form that was developed to serve that purpose.

The focus on all of the assessments should be to highlight student progress and to inform instruction. If students do not do as well as anticipated in a particular area, plans should be made to improve the work sessions in ways that will enable them to begin thinking about their own progress in becoming literate and to begin setting goals for their own improvement.

4

INSERVICE FOR
EDUCATIONAL ASSISTANTS

A rigorous inservice agenda should be an integral part of the Reading Club program. The inservice agenda should essentially focus on two areas: (1) successfully implementing The Reading Club and (2) continually expanding an understanding of literacy development with children.

The persons responsible for establishing The Reading Club in a particular school or district need to determine who will conduct the inservice sessions. It could be a classroom teacher, the reading specialist, or an outside reading expert. In the case of J. W. Riley and Hayes Two-Way Bilingual Schools, Dr. Kathryn Henn-Reinke from the University of Wisconsin, Oshkosh, conducted all of the inservice sessions, as she had a background in both reading and bilingual education. She also visited the sites on a regular basis to guide the work of the educational assistants. Generally, an inservice session was scheduled one time per month, for two to three hours per session. Some of the inservice topics are listed below:

- Overview of El Club de Lectura
- Outline of the testing process
- Stages of reading and writing
- Scheduling

- Student motivation/Positive approaches
- Strategy development
- Reviewing student progress/Pacing
- The writing process
- End-of-year celebrations

A brief overview of the content of these sessions may serve to generate ideas for conducting inservices. Sample agendas from actual inservices can be found in appendix G.

OVERVIEW OF THE READING CLUB

In the introductory workshop, educational assistants would benefit from learning how The Reading Club is organized. Having sample materials on hand and actually simulating the four components of a lesson (new book, word works, rereading, and writing) would give educational assistants a clearer sense of what these lessons should look like. Providing time for them to practice with the materials is essential. A small group of children might be brought in and a demonstration lesson conducted by the presenter. This allows the educational assistants to sit back and observe not only how the lessons are organized but also expectations for creating a positive but productive work environment. A second group of students might then be brought in and the educational assistants could actually try out the lesson format and receive feedback from the presenter. If at all possible, have the person who is to oversee this program present to guide the actual implementation of the program. Educational assistants may have worked in other programs and may need to sort out the difference between the expectations of this program and their former work. Or they may be new to this type of work and need support and assistance to begin work in the program. Also, there are always glitches in a new endeavor, and the coordinator can help solve many of them.

Time during the initial inservice sessions may be devoted to actual preparation of materials for the Reading Club lessons. To be ready for the start of The Reading Club, the following materials need to be prepared for use with the students: (1) alphabet letter cards for the word works section of the lesson; (2) several leveled books (8- or 16-page books for emergent readers that are leveled by the reading publisher from easiest to most difficult) starting with the level of the students and advancing three to four levels beyond the starting point of the students; and (3) writing journals for each student. In addition, it is very helpful to have a chalk/dry erase board, chalk or dry erase markers, writing utensils, and storage bins on hand for use during the lessons. The Reading Club can take place in the classroom *if* the space is quiet enough, well lighted, free of most distractions, and has sufficient work space. It is most efficient to have a secure space where the materials can be stored for easy access.

OUTLINE OF THE TESTING PROCESS

Either as part of the first inservice or, preferably, in a separate workshop, educational assistants need to learn how to conduct the initial student screening. This will be the first activity they will be engaged in with the students. Again, a simulation would work very well. A copy of testing materials can be found in appendix D. (An overview of the screening process can be found in chapter 3.)

Depending on how the program has been organized, part of this inservice session may also include actually preparing materials for the screening sessions. For testing, copies of the recording sheets must be run off for each child, and materials to be used by the child (alphabet card, word lists, and IRI story sheets) could be laminated. If leveled books are used, one book from each level should be selected and a recording sheet prepared for it. See appendix D for a sample miscue sheet.

STAGES OF READING AND WRITING

It is important for educational assistants to understand that there are stages of reading and writing that children progress through. The fact that children's reading and writing can be evaluated to determine the stage they are presently functioning at helps instructors make more realistic demands on students. Knowing the characteristics of the next stage provides educational assistants with valuable information about what to expect next from students. They can also gently nudge students to experiment with new skills and strategies as they appear ready for them. The stages of reading may be outlined in the following way:

Emergent Reader

- In this stage children begin to explore print.
- They look at the pictures to tell the story as they pretend read.
- They know some letters and sounds represented by the letters.
- They begin to recognize rhyming words.

Transitional Reader

- In this stage children begin to make sense of print and realize that the words tell the story.
- They begin to develop a sight-word vocabulary.
- They use pictures and some initial consonants to figure out new words.
- They begin to predict what the story will be about by looking at the pictures.
- They mainly read the story from memory after hearing it read numerous times.

Beginning Reader

- In this stage children understand that print tells the story and that they can use some strategies to help themselves read.
- They expand their sight-word vocabularies.
- They think about what would make sense in the story.
- They use sound/letter cues to figure out new words.
- They begin to self-correct mistakes.
- They use phonemic awareness more fully.

Advanced Beginning Reader

- In this stage children begin to use word analysis and comprehension strategies.
- They use chunking strategies to figure out new words.
- They monitor comprehension and self-correct errors.
- They discuss, retell, and/or apply what they have read.

Consolidating Reader

- In this stage children use word analysis and comprehension strategies efficiently and automatically.
- They read and comprehend in a variety of contexts.
- They increase their sight-word vocabularies.
- They refine their self-monitoring and self-correcting skills.

Accomplished Reader

- In this stage children read competently and efficiently in a variety of contexts.
- They use a variety of strategies appropriately and automatically.
- They expand their vocabularies on an ongoing basis.
- They develop strategies for comprehending complex text structures.

The stages of writing can be outlined in the following way:

Stage 1. Initially children do not distinguish between print and illustrations. They think they are "writing" when they draw.

Stage 2. At this stage, children scribble. They recognize that writing has to do with making lines on paper and that people can read back what they write. Young children scribble and then pretend to read what they have written.

Stage 3. At this stage, children begin to use some letter or letter-like figures. There is no correlation between the writing and what the child indicates the writing "says."

Stage 4. Actual letters begin to appear at this stage, often representing initial and/or final letters of words. A string of letters often stands for whole sentences. For example, "ILVMMom" might mean "I love my mom." Children begin to read back their writing to another person.

Stage 5. In this stage much of student writing can be easily read by another person, though many spelling irregularities still exist.

Stage 6. Standardized spelling and writing appear with greater frequency at this stage.

Samples of student writing may be evaluated periodically as a way for educational assistants to explore stages of writing more fully. In subsequent inservice sessions, actual writing samples from students in The

Reading Club may be reviewed to determine the kinds of improvements students are making. Goals may be set for guiding students to the next level in their writing. For example, if students are consistently using capital letters and periods, a next step might be to focus on writing about a single topic.

MOTIVATION/POSITIVE REINFORCEMENT

Many of the children who will be involved in The Reading Club will be children who do not have a very high opinion of their ability to be successful in school. Many will be functioning below most of their classmates and may not even have a very high level of self-esteem or self-confidence. Therefore, it is especially critical that The Reading Club be a very comfortable and positive experience for the children.

One of the first indicators that we notice when students begin to make progress with their literacy skills is that their attitude toward school begins to change. They become more energized and often even seem happier. For this to begin happening, students have to experience success, which is why the first lessons must be structured so students can easily complete them. As they get more and more of a taste of success, they feel more confident and are willing to take greater risks in their learning. As children begin to catch up to their peers in the classroom, they start to develop confidence in themselves as learners.

In this inservice, elements of creating a positive learning environment may be outlined. The importance of being open and welcoming to the children cannot be overemphasized. If an educational assistant is very strict with students, the difference between holding high expectations and making students feel comfortable and at ease in the sessions needs to be determined. It is also important that the educational assistant emphasize what the children *can* do instead of pointing out what they *cannot* do. Students' shortcomings should never be discussed in front of them. They hear these kinds of comments and take them to heart.

While creating a positive learning environment is of the utmost importance, high expectations must also be held for both behavior and literacy development in the Reading Club sessions. The children should know exactly what is expected of them from the very first day. The educational assistant and the children can collaboratively design a set of rules for behavior and work expectations, or the educational assistant can post a set of rules she/he designed. The work sessions are short, and the precedent must be set from the first sessions that there is not a minute to waste. If children do not follow the rules, consequences should be determined prior to the start of the sessions. We have run into very few behavior problems, but not allowing an unmotivated student to participate in the sessions for a day or two has been very effective.

Patience is an essential characteristic of those who work with children in The Reading Club. In some cases, struggling students have learned that if they do not know how to do the work but remain quiet, little will be expected of them. These students need to develop a work ethic by being gently made aware that they are expected to complete their work and to work hard every day. All or most of the students will need a little extra time and support to complete their work. Patience is critical here.

Motivation goes hand-in-hand with a positive learning environment. This is established in part by structuring learning experiences that children can complete successfully but that offer a manageable amount of challenge (instructional level). In this way children are not overwhelmed by work that is too difficult (frustration level) or are not moving forward with work that is too easy (independent level) for them.

If students are having some difficulty with the work or believe that they are not capable of completing it, efforts should be made to support their work. One component of support is to give students enough help so they can move forward on their own. When students are helped to do as much as possible for themselves, they begin to become independent learners.

SCHEDULING

After the students have been selected for inclusion in The Reading Club, the scheduling of sessions can begin. Generally, the principal or literacy coach will establish a meeting schedule for the various groups. A 45-minute session, four times per week is ideal. Educational assistants should post a schedule indicating the times and participants for each group. They may want to make certain the principal and the classroom teachers have copies of the schedule, as well.

It is very helpful for the principal to determine what, if any, activities educational assistants may be asked to complete instead of meeting with the Reading Club groups. These should be few in number, because groups that do not meet on a regular basis generally make little or no progress. At one of the inservice sessions, educational assistants should be advised of these exceptions and instructed as to what they should do if asked to take on other responsibilities during the scheduled Reading Club sessions.

Attendance for the students is equally important. We have found that excessive absences by students nearly always guarantee that they will not show progress in their literacy skills. At Hayes, the educational assistants take attendance every day. If students begin to miss school, they talk with them about the importance of being in school every day. When the students' attendance becomes more regular, the assistants point out how it improves their work. When attendance does not improve, they call the parents or talk with the administrators about possible interventions.

STRATEGY DEVELOPMENT

Strategy development should be an ongoing part of every inservice session. (See chapter 5 for a more in-depth overview of strategy development, including ideas for inservice sessions.) Determine the order in which the strategies are to be presented and developed. Simulated activities may be developed that enable the educational assistants to envision more clearly how the strategies might be taught and how they help students become more well-rounded readers.

As part of the inservice, educational assistants should share their efforts in trying to help students become more strategic readers. Successful attempts can be reinforced and suggestions made for less positive results. Ideas for reinforcing students' efforts to use strategies to get meaning from print could also be emphasized. For example, "I noticed that you looked at the picture when you got stuck on a word. Did that help you?" or "I noticed that when you got mixed up on that sentence, you read the whole sentence over again. That is a good strategy."

Once strategies have been introduced, it takes a great deal of practice before they become automatic for students. The process of helping them use these strategies more automatically in their reading is another good topic that can be revisited throughout the inservice sessions. Too often when children encounter a word that they do not know, the other children call it out or the teacher says, "Sound it out." Instead, educational assistants can learn how to turn these situations into learning opportunities for the children. Depending on the situation and the strategy that is being reinforced, the following prompts might be used for deciphering an unknown word:

- Does the picture help you here?
- Get your mouth ready to say the sound of the first letter.
- Look at the first letter and the picture.
- Are there any small words or clusters of letters that you know in the word?
- What would make sense here?
- Say "blank" for the word you don't know and read to the end of the sentence.
- What kind of word goes here (noun, verb)?
- Think about what you know about this topic and what would make sense here.

Children will need many reminders and lots of reinforcement in learning how to use these strategies in their reading. Stressing the importance of giving their classmates time to figure things out by themselves will be very helpful for students.

The same kinds of activities may be used when children do not comprehend a story or a part of a story. First, they should identify where they got confused. From there, the educational assistant could learn about teaching children to select the most appropriate strategies to use to help themselves figure out the passage, including:

- Do the pictures help you?
- What would make sense?
- Think about what you already know about this topic.
- Think about what you already know about this kind of story/book.

REVIEWING STUDENT PROGRESS/PACING

Student progress in literacy development is the main objective in The Reading Club. We want to move students along as quickly as possible in reading, writing, and use of strategies, without frustrating them. As soon as we see that students are reading very comfortably and successfully at a certain level, we want to move them to the next level. As soon as they master a particular skill in writing, we can add a new one. As soon as they use a particular strategy consistently, it is time to begin introducing a new one. Students should continue to get support wherever they need it, and if the pace is too fast, it should be adjusted to the instructional level of the students. The point is to keep students moving with confidence.

Review of student progress becomes very critical in this effort. During inservice sessions, educational assistants should examine samples of student work to share with one another and with the workshop facilitator. Judgments can be made about the content of the daily lessons; the pacing of reading, writing and word works components; and individual student strengths and challenges. After discussing these issues, decisions can be made about any changes that need to be made. The author visits the Club de Lectura sessions at Hayes and Riley on a regular basis, so most of the adjustments are made during those visits. Often the topic for inservice sessions originates from these visits, often because the educational assistants indicate that they would like some help in one area or another.

Many of the adjustments have to do with pacing. New books should not become "reread" books until they can be read with complete accuracy and confidence. Sometimes these books are moved too quickly to the "reread" portion of the session. In these cases it becomes simply a matter of moving one or two of the books back to "new book" status and making certain the students track the print with their fingers as they read. The same may happen with word works material, i.e., students are not completely familiar with the words before they are presented with a new set of words.

In writing, it may be that students are not making as much progress as would be expected. Upon closer examination, it may become evident that they are not being held responsible for following writing rules. It could also be that they are not expected to complete their writing on a regular basis and/or they never share their writing with anyone. The latter point is important because it gives students an audience to share their work with. If they get constructive feedback about their writing, they will be more likely to put greater effort into it. Sometimes, students are supplied with topics for writing on a regular basis. It is fine to do this occasionally, but students should select their own topics *most* of the time. Students write more fully on a topic that they care about. It also encourages independence in writing when they have control over what they write about.

Sometimes it happens that writing time gets skipped or shortened on a regular basis because it is the last activity of the session. In the beginning, the pace of the lessons should be adjusted so that all four activities (new book, word works, reread, and writing) take place every day. The beginning activities for first and second grades are very brief, and it is possible to do each of them on a daily basis. Once the students reach higher levels, it may be feasible to do two days of reading and two days of writing each week. Educational assistants may also consider changing the order of the lesson activities occasionally to devote equal attention to each of the components of the lesson.

As discussed in the chapter on assessment (chapter 3), teaching children to monitor and self-assess their own work is a huge step toward helping them become more independent in their learning. Inservice sessions need to focus on methods of teaching children to analyze their work to determine which skills and strategies they can use well and which ones they need to practice more. The educational assistants might also learn how to help children compare what they are doing now to work they completed earlier in the semester and discuss the growth.

Two goals targeted specifically for reading are that the students read fluently and that they read with comprehension. Assessing student progress in these areas could also become an inservice topic. Students might be asked to occasionally read aloud during the reread portion of the lesson. They have practiced these books and they should be very familiar with them. The educational assistant and the child could independently rate the reading fluency (for example, 3, very smooth and easy for the listener to follow; 2, fairly smooth and fairly easy for the listener to follow; or 1, not too smooth and not too easy for the listener to follow). If the child rates his/her fluency as too high or too low, the educational assistant can point out why that was not an accurate self-assessment and give the student pointers about how to judge the work more accurately the next time. Children who score a 2 or a 1 can set a goal to read more smoothly. They may wish to take the books home to practice before the next assessment. On subsequent ratings, discussions can be held about what improvements have been made in reading fluency. Children who score a 3 may try to read more challenging texts.

In terms of comprehension, inservice sessions may be devoted to training in monitoring and assessing students' understanding of what they've read. The easiest ways to do this are through use of questioning, "kid watching" (Wilde, 1996), and retelling. If questioning is used on a regular basis, educational assistants should be aware of the difference between lower-level questions that merely ask children to recall what they've read and higher-level questions that require children to really think about what they've read. A parallel skill for educational assistants to learn is how to ask questions that help students think about what they are reading but do not interrupt their concentration on the text. Assistants can also learn about how to observe children while they are reading (kid watching) and make informed judgments about how fully they are thinking about what they read. For example, if children react by laughing at funny parts or act surprised at unexpected things that happen to a character, they are probably engaged in the story. If they substitute incorrect words but these substitutions are logical to the story, this also indicates that they are thinking about what might happen next. Conversely, if they read words that are totally inappropriate for the story and do not self-correct them, it is a good indication that they are doing little thinking about what the reading passage is about, and they are merely reading the words. Asking children to retell stories is another assessment tool for comprehension. Educational assistants could participate in training activities aimed at modeling and assessing retelling. The same process suggested for self-assessing fluency could be used by having the educational assistant and the child independently rate the accuracy and conciseness of a story retelling and then comparing the results. The rating scale might look like the one in figure 4.1.

A. In my retelling, I included:

____ all of the important
information. (3)

____ some of the important
information. (2)

____ only a little of the important
information. (1)

B. In my retelling, I included:

____ none of the unimportant
details. (3)

____ some of the unimportant
details. (2)

____ lots of unimportant
details. (1)

Figure 4.1. Self-Assessment of Story Retelling.

THE WRITING PROCESS

Although the amount of time allotted for writing in The Reading Club is fairly limited, steps can still be taken to help children progress in their writing ability. Teaching writing as a process in which writers organize their ideas, write a draft, edit and revise their draft, and write a final copy highlights that the purpose of writing is to communicate clearly with the reader. If the writing process is being taught in the classroom, the same format could be used for The Reading Club. In this way, the students will have additional opportunities to become familiar with writing expectations of the classroom.

Brainstorming writing topics and organizing ideas before writing are two components of prewriting. As discussed earlier, many Reading Club students are reluctant to write because it is so challenging for them. Initially, the educational assistant may keep a chart of writing ideas generated by the students. Each day new ideas may be added to the chart. Students who have ideas to write about should be encouraged to begin writing. Students who cannot think of a writing topic could search the listing (or have it read to them) for a possible topic. If none of these topics are appealing, talk with the student(s) about possible ideas: "Do you have a pet? Write about what you do after school. Did you go to any fun places? You could write about your family."

Sometimes the child needs a couple of minutes to mull the ideas over and then will begin to write. Occasionally, it is necessary to set a deadline for getting some writing done. This should be a last resort, as it could make writing seem like a chore while the goal is for children to come to see reading and writing as enjoyable pursuits.

Once the children can independently select a topic for their writing, the educational assistant may focus on having children organize their ideas prior to writing. We described the use of the Power Writing organizer in chapter 2, *Shared/Independent Writing* and idea maps (refer back to figure 2.5) for helping children brainstorm and sequence their ideas for writing. For younger children, it may be helpful to just chat with them before they start writing. This often helps them expand the number of details they might include in their story. For example, if a child wanted to write about her dog, the educational assistant might say, "Tell me all about your dog." If the child volunteers little information, additional questions might be posed. "What does your dog look like? What does he like to do? Who takes care of the dog? Where did you get him?"

After the children generate ideas for their topic, they might number them in the order they will write about them. This really helps them think about a logical way to sequence their writing. Even if emergent writers only write one sentence about each idea, they can still determine what should be first, second, and third.

Donald Graves (1994) urges children to just write and get their ideas down on paper, without worrying too much about correctness during the first draft. Though students should be reminded of the writing rules they have studied so far, it is important for them to concentrate on their ideas for writing during the draft. Remind students to use their prewriting organizer to help them remember what they planned to write about. There are some additional writing aids that students could be exposed to in this stage. For instance, teach them to use a caret to add a word or phrase. They also might benefit from simply crossing out words and phrases they want to change or delete rather than erasing, as it takes less time and does not usually result in ripped papers.

Once a draft has been completed, students move to the editing stage. They should read the draft to themselves two times; once to make sure the ideas sound right and a second time to check for mechanics. Children should point to each word as they read because inexperienced writers often leave out words. By pointing to each word they are more likely to notice when a word or phrase is missing. It is very helpful to use a different-colored pencil for the editing phase. When they reread for mechanics, make sure they are reminded of the writing rules they have studied so far. Writers can have the list of writing rules in front of them.

Children may ask another member of the group to read the writing and give them feedback as well. If peer editing is used, have them look for very specific aspects of writing. For example, they may begin by looking only for capital letters and then include punctuation, sentence variety, etc., as they become more skilled at writing. Help children determine whether they think the writing is interesting or how it could be made more interesting. A peer-editing checklist (see appendix F) could be developed from the writing rules. Peer editors might offer suggestions about what is clear or unclear and what they wanted to hear more about from the writer. However, it is up to the author to determine which changes in content she/he wishes to make. Not all writing pieces need to be edited so completely.

The student then writes a final draft of the writing piece. Final drafts of some of the writing pieces may be written or typed on special paper for display or to share with others. The educational assistant should also edit pieces that will be made public in any way, and the final draft should be as error free as possible. If wall space is available, it is a good practice to display students' writing as a way of encouraging them to take pride in their work. Other final drafts can be kept in the students' writing folders and periodically reviewed to monitor progress. It is important to date all writing materials so students can put them in chronological order for reviewing their progress.

END-OF-YEAR CELEBRATIONS

Each year the Hayes Two-Way Bilingual School hosts an end-of-year celebration for all of the students. It is a brief party of about one hour that serves as an opportunity to showcase the students' progress and to encourage them to continue reading and writing during the summer.

All students in El Club de Lectura are invited. Samples of student writing from each group are displayed on large posters. One or two children are asked to share a brief story that they can read fluently. Occasionally, the educational assistants turn one of the books into a play and perform it for the children. The children seem to really enjoy this.

The principal gives a brief talk about the students' hard work and how much progress they have made and then awards each of them a Club de Lectura certificate and a small gift. The celebration ends with a special cake and refreshments. Pictures from each year are added to the Club de Lectura scrapbook, which is put on display during the party. Many of the students make tremendous progress in the span of a single academic year. The celebration is simple, but it is important to take advantage of every possible opportunity to recognize students' efforts and to encourage them to continue working hard.

5

STRATEGY DEVELOPMENT

Good readers use a variety of strategies to help them make sense of what they are reading (Routman, 2000). Teaching students in The Reading Club to use strategies is an important part of the program. For this reason a separate chapter has been devoted to strategy development. The strategies are addressed from the perspective of the educational assistant learning to teach strategies and the student learning to use strategies to improve reading comprehension. Inservicing educational assistants about strategies should be thought of as an ongoing endeavor. Most educational assistants have had little formal training in teaching reading and writing. And most use a phonics approach when children encounter a word they do not know because that is the way they learned to read. "Sound it out" is what children are told to do.

This is a good strategy that can be very helpful in lots of situations. But there are many other strategies students can use to figure out new words and comprehend a text more fully. When children get fairly good at using strategies, they may even use two or more at the same time, e.g., look at the first letter, look at the picture, and think about what would make sense.

Developing strategies is probably the most crucial aspect of The Reading Club, because it helps children build a repertoire of aids that they can use to support their own reading. However, it is also the area where educational assistants generally need the most training, support, and practice.

The most effective method that we have found is to introduce one strategy during an inservice session. The educational assistants try them out with the children and then evaluate how well the particular strategy is being implemented. If the coordinator of the program is able, it would be beneficial to have him/her model using the strategy with the children. The educational assistants can then try working with the strategy. Regular visits to Reading Club sites can also help ensure that the strategies are being used correctly and consistently. These are the reading strategies that we focus on most fully:

- Picture clues
- Previewing text/Prediction
- Context clues: What would make sense here?
- Reading to the end of the sentence/Rereading
- Phonics/Sounding out words
- Prior knowledge
- Self-correction

PICTURE CLUES

We always lead off with teaching children to use picture clues, because they are the easiest for students to manage and for educational assistants to teach. Also, because we start off with very basic predictable books, pictures are a very dominant feature of each book. A first step is to select some books being used that would be good samples for teaching picture clues. For example, books that contain sentences such as "Lions can run fast. Giraffes can run fast. Bears can run fast" are useful for this purpose. The students should be instructed to look at the picture to help them know which animal will be named next.

A next step might be to have the educational assistants work on using picture clues *and* the sound of the first letter of the word to figure out a word. Children do not look at the individual letters of a word or clusters of letters when they first begin to read. They look only at the first letter of the word. If they are at this stage, it makes sense to focus on the initial letter and work on other word parts a bit later.

Getting students to use the strategies consistently is a huge part of the instructional process. The inservice sessions should provide opportunities to reinforce this concept. It can be presented as a three-step process: (1) teach the strategy, (2) assist children in using the strategy, and (3) reinforce student use of the strategies in independent reading.

Educational assistants might wish to cover a word in a story that has a corresponding picture clue. The introduction to the strategy might look something like this:

1. "When we come to a word we don't know, we can look at the picture to see if it can help us out. Let's say that we don't know the first word in the sentence '_____ can run fast.'"
2. "Can the picture help us? What is in the picture?" "Yes. Lions. What does the sentence say?" "Yes. Lions can run fast."
3. As a student reads and gets stuck, remind him/her to see if the pictures can help. "Very good, Juan, I noticed that when you were not sure of that word you looked at the picture for help."

PREVIEWING TEXT/PREDICTION

Children should look at the cover and the title of a new book and make a prediction about what the story might be about. This is a good way to get them thinking about what they will be reading. Next, have the children page through the book and discuss what they see in the pictures and what they think the story will be about.

During inservice sessions, educational assistants might preview two or three of the children's books and determine which one has pictures that give the best indication of what the book will be about. It is important to select a book that tells the story clearly from the pictures to begin teaching this strategy. Simulation activities can be used to give educational assistants an opportunity to practice teaching children to preview text.

At other times, when the book contains a surprise partway through the text, educational assistants will not want to have the children preview the pages. Instead they will have the children make a prediction before they turn the page. Then the students turn the page and read to see whether or not their prediction was correct. Again, predicting and then checking on the accuracy of the prediction is a process for taking meaning from print.

Inservice sessions might focus on the importance of previewing books prior to using them with children. Books that will be used by the children can be reviewed to determine whether to have them peruse all of the pages prior to reading or whether to have them predict before seeing the next page. In both instances the importance of making and confirming predictions should be stressed.

CONTEXT CLUES: WHAT WOULD MAKE SENSE HERE?

Using context clues is another way to engage students in thinking about what they are reading. When children come to a word they do not know or do not understand, they should check to see if there are any clues in the rest of the sentence that can help them out. For example, let's say a child does not know the word "years" in the passage "Today is Jonathan's birthday. He is 6 _____ old." From the other words in the sentence, the child can probably figure out the word "years" because it makes sense in the context.

For the inservices dealing with using context clues, a number of examples of using context clues can be prepared for review by the educational assistants. Key words can be covered up and they can practice how they would teach children to use the context clues to figure out the missing or unknown word. There are two more difficult challenges in this strategy. The first is to refrain from saying to children, "Sound it out," and instead work with children to use context clues to figure out the word. The second is to make certain there are sufficient context clues children could use to figure out an unknown word. We cannot ask them to use context clues if there are none in the sentence that could help them. Educational assistants might prepare to teach context clues in the following way:

- Select some good examples for use of context clues, covering up the key word.
- Ask children to read the sentence and guess the covered word.

- Ask children, "Does your guess make sense?"
- Have children share what clues they used to make a guess.
- Review clues with the children.
- Remind students to use the strategy when they get stuck.
- Point out whenever it is noted that students used the strategy in their reading.

READING TO THE END OF THE SENTENCE/REREADING

This strategy is an extension of the context-clue strategy discussed above. When students come to a word they do not know and cannot figure out, they may skip the word and read to the end of the sentence. Or if they get confused in reading a sentence, they may reread the sentence to see if they can now make sense of what they read. Educational assistants can practice these strategies in an inservice and then try them out with their students.

PHONICS/SOUNDING OUT WORDS

On a daily basis, students are practicing with letters, sounds, and word parts in the Word Works section of the Reading Club lessons. When students study elements of phonics, the purpose is to apply them to their reading. An inservice on phonics could focus on making links between what was studied in the Word Works session and actual reading.

For example, let's say the rhyming words *fast, last, past* had been studied previously and now the children are stuck on the word *cast* in the sentence "Jayme's arm is in a cast." Children can be reminded that they have studied words that rhymed with this one. Ask them to cover up the /c/ and see if they can recall or sound out the rime "ast." In another example, the unknown word is "fame" and the students have already studied e-marker words. The students can be reminded that this is an e-marker word and encouraged to use that information to figure the word out. If students don't remember the e-marker pattern, a quick review would tell them that often when words end with *e* the vowel that comes in the middle of the word will say its own name (or be a long vowel).

PRIOR KNOWLEDGE

Sometimes children don't recognize that they know something about the topic they are reading about and need opportunities to explore what they already know. Inservice sessions should focus on encouraging children to discuss the topic while making predictions about new stories. Also, when students are stuck, asking students "What would make sense here?" guides them to think about what they already know.

SELF-CORRECTION

The major goal of The Reading Club is to develop readers who read well and who comprehend what they read. One of the indicators that children are doing this is that they self-correct their own reading errors.

Educational assistants can be asked to record errors the children make in reading aloud, as well as the kinds of self-corrections they make. At an inservice session the errors and self-corrections can be analyzed to determine (1) which errors indicate a break in comprehension and which reflect concentration on the topic and (2) what the self-corrections show about comprehension.

Inservice sessions should frequently reflect on the importance of reinforcing student use of strategies. Whenever educational assistants notice students using strategies they should point it out. Or if children appear to be stuck and then figure out the word or phrase, they should ask "What did you do to figure that out?" or "What strategy did you use to figure that out?" During inservice sessions, ask educational assistants to share how they reinforce use of strategies and how students respond. When children can help themselves and can describe how they helped themselves, we call that "metacognition." We want students to know things and to know how they know things. When they can name the strategies they use, we know that they indeed understand the strategies.

As pointed out in the assessment chapter (chapter 3), students should be given opportunities to self-assess their use of strategies in their reading. Inservice sessions could focus on which strategies to highlight and how to organize the self-assessment process. Obviously, only the strategies that have been taught should be assessed. If picture clues have been taught, children could be asked how well they used picture clues by marking the appropriate face (happy, so-so, or sad). Or educational assistants could ask children to show them where they used pictures in the story to help them with the words. The same could be done with predicting or using context clues.

After students have been introduced to several strategies, they could use the chart in figure 3.6 for self-assessment. The educational assistants could let the children know if they agree with their self-assessments of their use of strategies. Children who are not using strategies or not moving forward in their use of strategies should get extra attention. Inservice sessions could focus on options for working on this issue. For example, during the reread time, the educational assistant could read with one or two students who need work on specific strategies.

When students have learned several strategies, they will often use more than one at a time. For example, in the sentence quoted earlier, "Jayme's arm is in a cast," figuring out the word *cast* may involve use of context clues, picture clues, and phonics clues. Children should think about whether the word makes sense to the story. If it does, they should continue reading. If it does not, they should revisit the sentence to try to make sense of it. Sometimes it is a good strategy to just skip a word and continue reading, if all else makes sense. And after all, making sense of what they read is the major goal.

6

EXITING THE PROGRAM

The personnel involved in overseeing The Reading Club will need to establish guidelines and criteria for children who are ready to exit the program. The decision to exit the program is best made by more than one person to make certain the child is truly ready to end their membership in The Reading Club.

Occasionally, teachers note the progress of one or more of the children in The Reading Club and realize that now there are other children in the classroom who are further behind and in greater need of assistance. The temptation may exist to exchange students in this situation, but this is generally not advisable. Although the students may be demonstrating wonderful progress, they need time to solidify the skills and strategies they have learned. The individualized support they receive in The Reading Club will not be available to the same degree in the classroom.

We generally keep the students in The Reading Club until they have reached grade level (as determined by classroom Reading Verification measures) and maintained that level for a few weeks. The attitude of the student plays a role in making the decision, also. By the time students reach grade-level literacy expectations, they should be completing classroom assignments with accuracy and confidence.

Some of the measures that may be used as criteria for exiting The Reading Club might include:

- Completion of the Reading Club screening test with grade-level results.
- Review of skills and strategies used independently by the student.
- Grade-level measure(s) of reading and writing ability from the classroom.
- Review of level of student confidence in reading and writing.

If children regress once they return to the classroom and no longer have the additional support, they may be returned to The Reading Club for a time. If they appear to do well in the classroom, their spots may be filled by other struggling readers.

It is advisable to have students complete the screening test before they leave the program, so that exit data is available for reviewing student progress in order to make the decision about whether or not the child is ready to exit the program. It is also helpful to monitor the progress of the students for as long as they are in the school to determine if they are able to maintain their ability to do grade-level work. Some students may need additional supports as they move into more complex content area subjects at about third or fourth grade.

Most of the students whom we work with are able to exit the program after about eight or nine months. Often students who do not exit the program within a single academic year are also students who have attendance issues and/or more severe learning problems than originally anticipated.

A

EL CLUB DE LECTURA/THE READING CLUB FOR KINDERGARTEN

The kindergarten plan is designed for K–5 students who are struggling with learning their letters and sounds, attending to literacy-related activities in the classroom, and/or retelling stories. It is intended for use during the latter part of the school year, after students have had extended exposure to these concepts in the classroom. The plan entails 30 minutes of intervention activities per day to strengthen students' literacy skills before they enter first grade.

The kindergarten plan may be made more or less challenging depending on the needs of the children. If children are seriously struggling, it may be necessary to focus on only one or two letters per week, at least initially. More games and activities could be built around these letters and sounds to make certain that children learn them fully.

The format of the lessons is somewhat similar to the Reading Club lessons for first and second grades. A maximum of four students should be included in each group. Ideally groups would meet on a daily basis, as we have found meeting only one or two days per week to be quite ineffective. Greater emphasis is placed on letter recognition and initial sounds in the kindergarten lessons. Children read every day and write journal entries one or two times per week. Each day students practice writing the letters they have learned.

The students begin each session by working with the new letter(s) and sounds for the week. Initially, the educational assistant presents the letter and the students repeat the name of the letters. After students know the letters fairly well, the educational assistant can give the sound of the letter and the students can identify the corresponding letter. Still later, the educational assistant may ask for the letters heard at the beginning of a word. If at all possible, use magnetic or three-dimensional letters to enable students to feel the shapes of the letters. Games and activities are suggested to give children more opportunities to learn the sounds and letters. During each two-week segment, students begin with the uppercase form of the new letters and add the lowercase letters in the second week.

The students then search for new letters and sounds in the books they are reading. For example, if a new letter is *j*, students can search for that letter in the book. Or the educational assistant may direct the children to look at the pictures to see if they can find anything that begins with the /j/ sound. The educational assistant may direct the children to a certain page, say the name of a word that begins with a certain letter being studied, and ask the children to find the word.

Each day includes a reading of the new book and rereading of previously read books. As in the format for the older children, preview the new book and have the children make predictions. Children should also track the print with their fingers. During each two-week plan there are activities that focus on comprehension. Students are asked to retell stories, act them out, identify characters, or identify favorite pictures. The main focus is to get children to enjoy the books and to begin building a sight-word vocabulary.

Letter-formation practice occurs nearly every day. This is essentially a penmanship activity in which students learn how to practice writing the letters they have learned so far. Children learn to form the letters correctly and receive additional practice in recognizing the letters of the alphabet.

One or two days per week, the penmanship practice may be replaced by journal-writing activities. Children should be encouraged to write on a topic of their own choosing and share it with the group or a partner when they are finished. The main focus of the journal entries should be to get children writing on their own. It is not the time for insisting on correct spelling. Educational assistants may guide children to think about the first letter in words while they are writing. Many children will be at the emergent stage of writing, so their first writing samples may be mostly scribbles or random letters. With practice, their writing will begin to improve.

EL CLUB DE LECTURA: KINDER

Semanas 1 y 2

A. Letras
1. Presentar las letras nuevas: *Aa, Bb, Cc, Dd, Oo, Zz*
   - Aquí tenemos la letra ___.
   - ¿Qué letra tenemos aquí?
2. Reconocer las letras
   - Dar letras a los niños.
   - Enséñame la letra ___.
3. Letras y sonidos (usando las láminas del cuento)
   - ¿Qué sonido oímos al principio de ___?
   - Enséñame esta letra.
4. Formar letras
   - El/la ayudante escribe las letras (una por una) en la pizarra.
   - Los niños escriben las letras de la semana en sus pizarritas.

B. Lectura libro 1—de nivel kinder
1. Los niños escuchan y siguen el cuento con el/la ayudante leyendo
2. Escuchar y repetir lo que lee el/la ayudante
3. Leer juntos
4. Buscar palabras y letras
   - Busca la letra en el cuento.
   - Busca una palabra que empiece con la letra.
   - Busca una palabra que rima.

C. ¿Cuál es tu lámina favorita en este cuento? (se usa durante semana 2)
D. Una o dos veces por semana (durante semana 2) los niños escriben en sus diarios en vez de formar letras.

Semanas 3 y 4

A. Letras
1. Presentar las letras nuevas: *Hh, Jj, Mm, Ss, Uu, Ee, Nn* (mayúsculas durante semana 3: mayúsculas y minúsculas durante semana 4)
   - Aquí tenemos la letra ___.
   - ¿Qué letra tenemos aquí?
   - Revisar las letras de semanas 1 y 2: *Aa, Bb, Cc, Dd, Oo, Zz*.

   2. Reconocer las letras
- Juntando las letras (Lotería)—letras mayúsculas en semana 3 y minúsculas también en semana 4.

   3. Letras y sonidos
- ¿Qué sonido oímos al principio de ___?

   4. Formar letras
- El/la ayudante escribe las letras (una por una) en la pizarra.
- Los niños escriben las letras en papel con crayolas.

B. Lectura libro 2—de nivel kinder
   1. Escuchar y seguir
- Hablar de los dibujos.

   2. Escuchar y repetir
   3. Leer juntos
   4. Buscar palabras y letras
- Busca la letra en el cuento.
- Busca una palabra que empiece con la letra.
- Busca una palabra que rima.

C. Leer en revisa libro 1
D. Relatar lo que pasa en el cuento (semana 4)
E. Una o dos veces por semana los niños escriben en sus diarios en vez de formar letras.

Semanas 5 y 6

A. Letras
   1. Presentar las letras nuevas: *Ff, Ii, Ll ll, Pp, Rr, Tt, Vv*
- Aquí tenemos la letra ___.
- ¿Qué letra tenemos aquí? (Mayúsculas durante semana 5, mayúsculas y minúsculas durante semana 6).
- Aquí tenemos la letra ___.
- ¿Qué letra tenemos aquí?
- Revisar las letras de semanas 1 y 2: *Aa, Bb, Cc, Dd, Oo, Zz.*
- Revisar las letras de semanas 3 y 4: *Hh, Jj, Mm, Ss, Uu, Ee, Nn.*

   2. Reconocer las letras
- Pescando para letras mayúsculas (semana 5).
- Pescando para letras mayúsculas y minúsculas (semana 6).

3. Letras y sonidos (usando las láminas del cuento)
   - Escuchan a la palabra.
   - Escriben la primera letra en las pizarritas.
4. Formar letras
   - El/la ayudante escribe las letras (una por una) en la pizarra.
   - Los niños escriben las letras con tiza.

B. Lectura libro 3—de nivel kinder
   1. Escuchar y seguir
   2. Escuchar y repetir
   3. Leer juntos
   4. Buscar letras, sonidos y palabras que riman
C. Leer en revisa
   1. Libro 1
   2. Libro 2
D. Los niños identifican los personajes de los cuentos ya leídos (semana 6)
E. Una o dos veces por semana los niños escriben en sus diarios en vez de formar letras (semana 6).

Semanas 7 y 8

A. Letras
   1. Presentar las letras nuevas: *Gg, Kk, Qq, Ww, Xx, Yy, Ññ*
      - Aquí tenemos la letra ___. (Mayúsculas durante semana 7, mayúsculas y minúsculas durante la semana 8).
      - ¿Qué letra tenemos aquí?
      - Revisar las letras ya estudiadas.
   2. Reconocer las letras
      - Pescando para letras mayúsculas durante semana 7.
      - Pescando para letras mayúsculas y minúsculas durante semana 8.
      - Juntando las letras para formar palabras.
   3. Letras y sonidos (usando las láminas) de los cuentos
      - Escuchan a la palabra.
      - Escriben la primera letra en las pizarritas.
   4. Formar letras
      - El/la ayudante escribe las letras (una por una) en la pizarra.
      - Los niños escriben las letras con marcadoras.

B. Lectura libro 4—de nivel kinder
   1. Escuchar y seguir
   2. Escuchar y repetir
   3. Leer juntos
   4. Buscar palabras y letras
C. Leer en revisa
   1. Libro 1
   2. Libro 2
   2. Libro 3
D. Los niños hacen dramas con los cuentos ya leídos (semana 8).
E. Una o dos veces por semana los niños escriben en sus diarios en vez de formar letras (semana 8).

READING CLUB: KINDERGARTEN

Weeks I and 2

A. Letters
   1. Introduce the new letters: *Aa, Bb, Cc, Dd, Mm, Ss*
     • Week 1: Introduce uppercase letters.
     • Week 2: Introduce uppercase and lowercase letters.
   2. Letter recognition: Give letter tiles/cards to the children
     • Week 1: Ask, "Who has the letter —?"
     • Week 2: Students match upper and lowercase letters.
   3. Letters and sounds (using story pictures)
     • What sound do you hear at the beginning of the word _____?
     • Show me the letter that you hear in that word.
   4. Letter-formation practice
     • Educational assistant teaches students to write the new letters one by one.
     • The children write the letters for the week on individual chalkboards.
B. Read kindergarten-level book 1
   1. Children listen and follow along while educational assistant reads the book
   2. The educational assistant reads and the children repeat

3. Read together
4. Letter and word searches
   - Find the letter ___ in one of the words in your story.
   - Find a word that starts with the letter ___ .
   - Find a word that rhymes with ___ .
C. What is your favorite picture in book 1? (ask in week 2)
D. One or two times per week students complete a journal entry in place of letter formation practice (week 2).

Weeks 3 and 4

A. Letters
   1. Introduce the new letters: *Gg, Ii, Kk, Ll, Rr*
   2. Letter recognition
      - Practice letter matching (memory game) with new letters (uppercase in week 3).
      - Students match upper and lowercase letters for weeks 1–4.
      - Review letters from weeks 1 and 2: *Aa, Bb, Cc, Dd, Mm, Ss*
   3. Letters and sounds (using pictures from story)
      - What sound do you hear at the beginning of the word —?
      - Show me the letter that you hear in that word.
   4. Letter-formation practice
      - Educational assistant teaches students to write the new letters one by one.
      - Write the letters for the week with crayons on small rolls of paper.
B. Read kindergarten-level book 2
   1. Children listen and follow along while the educational assistant reads
   2. The educational assistant reads and the children repeat
   3. Read book together
   4. Do letter and word searches
      - Find the letter ___ in one of the words in your story.
      - Find a word that starts with the letter ___ .
      - Find a word that rhymes with ___ .
C. Reread book 1
D. Tell what this book was about (week 4)

E. One or two times per week students complete a journal entry in place of letter-formation practice (week 4).

Weeks 5 and 6

A. Letters
   1. Introduce the new letters: *Ee, Ff, Hh, Nn, Uu, Oo, Qq*
   2. Letter recognition
      • Fish for letters (uppercase in week 5; upper and lowercase in week 6). (Place paper clips on each letter. A string with a magnet at the end forms the "pole.")
      • Review letters from weeks 1–4: *Aa, Bb, Cc, Dd, Mm, Ss, Gg, Ii, Kk, Ll, Rr.*
   3. Letters and sounds (using story pictures)
      • Listen to new word.
      • Show me the letter that you hear at the beginning of that word.
      • Point to word in the book.
   4. Letter-formation practice
      • Educational assistant teaches students to write the new letters one by one.
      • Students write the letters for the week on individual chalkboards.
B. Read kindergarten-level book 3
   1. Listen and follow along
   2. Read and repeat
   3. Read together
   4. Letter and word searches
      • Find the letter ___ in one of the words in your story.
      • Find a word that starts with the letter ___.
      • Find a word that rhymes with ___.
      • Find a picture in the story that starts with the letter___.
C. Reread
   1. Book 1
   2. Book 2
D. Name characters in the stories you have read so far (week 6)
E. One or two times per week students complete a journal entry instead of penmanship practice (week 6)

Weeks 7 and 8

A. Letters
1. Introduce the new letters: *Jj, Pp, Vv, Ww, Xx, Yy, Zz*
2. Letter recognition
   - Fish for letters (uppercase in week 7; upper and lowercase in week 8).
   - Review letters from weeks 1–6: Letter matching (upper/lowercase).
3. Letters and sounds (using story pictures)
   - Listen to new word.
   - Write first letter on chalkboards.
   - Compare letter to word card.
4. Letter-formation practice
   - Educational assistant teaches students to write the new letters one by one.
   - Students write the letters for the week with shaving cream.
B. Read kindergarten-level book 4
1. Listen and follow along
2. Read and repeat
3. Read together
4. Letter and word searches
   - Find the letter ___ in one of the words in your story.
   - Find a word that starts with the letter ___.
   - Find a word that rhymes with ___.
C. Reread
1. Book 1
2. Book 2
3. Book 3
D. Act out the stories read so far (week 8)
E. One or two times per week students complete a journal entry (week 8)

B

EL CLUB DE LECTURA/THE READING CLUB: FOURTH-GRADE SOCIAL STUDIES

El Club de Lectura/The Reading Club may be used in fourth and fifth grades only with significant modifications. At these grade levels the content-area requirements have become much more extensive. Therefore, as we experimented with a design for El Club de Lectura at Hayes Bilingual School, it became very clear that one of the subject areas should be used as the focus. We opted to design the program around social studies at both grade levels.

The teachers at each grade level determined the focus areas to be developed during these lessons. These areas were selected in relation to the Wisconsin State Reading and Social Studies Standards. Fourth-grade teachers wanted their students to be able to identify main ideas, use graphic organizers to represent information, and compare/contrast ideas. The social studies series being used at Hayes Bilingual School lent itself well to this purpose. There was an emphasis on developing thinking skills, social studies reading skills, and strategies already present in the series. The goal was to have students learn these skills and strategies to strengthen both their reading and their social studies abilities.

Although the format was somewhat repetitive, students began to look forward to these sessions. Having the educational assistant read the passages to the students first enabled them to concentrate on the content without having to struggle with reading the text also. Additional activities provided them with opportunities to solidify their understanding of content and vocabulary. Discussing responses orally first enabled students to develop better understanding of concepts before they were required to write them. A trade book was also selected as a read-aloud at each grade level. The book selected further expanded the topic under study in the social studies text.

It took a few weeks before students had built a base for reading and understanding social studies texts. But once they had developed some background in both areas, they began to move along at a faster rate. As much as possible, the Club de Lectura groups at these grade levels paralleled what the teachers were teaching in social studies with the rest of the class.

Focus Areas

- Graphic organizers
- Main idea
- Compare/contrast

Materials Needed

- Journal for each student
- Maps from teacher guide
- Vocabulary word cards

CHAPTER 1: THE GREAT LAKES REGION

Section 1: The Great Lakes

1. Preview the pages for section 1 (or first four or five pages). What do you think these pages will be about?
   - Look at headings.
   - Look at pictures and captions.
   - Name the Great Lakes (HOMES).
   - Why do you think they are important?
   - Locate the Great Lakes on the map.
2. Develop two or three questions that focus on the main ideas of the section. (The classroom teacher might want to supply these questions.)

- Students write questions in journals.
- Discuss possible answers.

Vocabulary

1. Write key vocabulary words (often highlighted in texts) and sentences from text using vocabulary terms in journals.
   - Draw pictures when possible.
   - Make word cards for key vocabulary terms.
   - Students add two or three words they did not know (after reading).
   - Use vocabulary word cards to review definitions.

Read

1. Day 1: Educational assistant reads section 1 to students, and they listen for main ideas.
   - Discuss answers to questions for journals.
   - Write answers for each question.
2. Day 2: Students read in pairs.
   - Students write main ideas from section 1 in journals as questions. For example: What are the names of the Great Lakes? Why are the Great Lakes important? How are the Great Lakes and the Mississippi River connected? How did businesses help one another?
   - Students ask one another questions each day.

Maps

1. Students paste copy of map of North America in journals.
   - Find and label the Great Lakes.
   - Find and label the United States and Canada.
   - Find and label large cities along the Great Lakes (Chicago, Gary, Cleveland, Buffalo, Sault Sainte Marie).
   - Find and label manufacturing cities along the Great Lakes (Gary [steel], Detroit [autos], etc.).

Read aloud from **Tom Sawyer.**

Section 2: Rivers of the Midwest

1. Preview section 2: What do you think these pages will be about?
   - Look at headings.
   - Look at pictures and captions.

- Look at charts and graphs.
- Map of Upper Midwest: How can you tell where rivers are on a map? Where is the Mississippi and why is it important? What other rivers can you find?

2. Develop two or three questions that focus on the main ideas of the section.
   - Students write questions in journals.
   - Discuss possible answers.

Vocabulary

1. Write key vocabulary words and sentences from text using vocabulary words in journals.
   - Draw pictures when possible.
   - Make word cards for key vocabulary terms.
   - Write a definition on the back of the card.
2. Students add two or three words they did not know (after reading).
3. Use vocabulary word cards to review definitions.

Read

1. Day 1: Educational assistant reads to students, and they listen for main ideas.
   - Discuss answers to questions for journals.
   - Write answers for each question.
2. Day 2: Students read in pairs.
   - Students write main ideas from section 2 in journals as questions.
   - Students ask one another questions each day.

Maps of the Mississippi region

1. Find and label the Mississippi, Ohio, and Missouri Rivers.
2. Find and label the Appalachian Mountains and New Orleans.

Read aloud from Tom Sawyer.

Section 3: More Rivers in the United States

1. Preview section 3: What do you think these pages will be about?
   - Look at headings.
   - Look at pictures and captions.
   - Look at maps.

2. Develop two or three questions that focus on the main ideas of the section.
   - Students write questions in journals.
   - Discuss possible answers.

Vocabulary

1. Write key vocabulary words and sentences in journals.
   - Draw pictures when possible.
   - Make word cards for key vocabulary terms.
   - Write definition on the back.
2. Students add two or three words they did not know (after reading).
3. Use vocabulary word cards to review definitions.

Read

1. Day 1: Educational assistant reads to students, and they listen for main ideas.
   - Discuss answers to questions for journals.
   - Write answers for each question.
2. Day 2: Students read in pairs.
   - Students write main ideas from section 3 in journals as questions.
   - Students ask one another questions each day.
   - Review and discuss charts and other graphics. What do the graphics tell us?

Maps of rivers in the U.S.

1. Locate the Mississippi River and label the source and the mouth of the Mississippi.
2. Find and label major cities along the Mississippi River.
3. Find and label other major rivers in the United States.

Read aloud from **Tom Sawyer.**

CHAPTER 2: ONE COUNTRY, MANY PARTS

Section 1: Landforms of the United States

1. Preview section 1: What do you think these pages will be about?
   - Look at headings: How do areas differ in the U.S.?
   - Look at pictures and captions.
   - What do the maps and graphics in this section tell us?

2. Develop two or three questions that focus on the main ideas of the section.
   - Students write questions in journals.
   - Discuss possible answers.

Vocabulary

1. Write key vocabulary words and sentences in journals.
   - Draw pictures for each landform and add a description (mountains, hills, plateaus, plains), looking for clues in words, e.g., *plate*au—a plate is flat.
2. Make word cards for key vocabulary terms.
   - Write a definition on the back of each vocabulary card.
3. Students add two or three words they did not know (after reading).
4. Use vocabulary word cards to review definitions.

Read

1. Day 1: Educational assistant reads section 1 to students, and they listen for main ideas.
   - Discuss answers to questions for journals.
   - Write answers for each question.
2. Day 2: Students read in pairs.
   - Students write main ideas in journals as questions.
   - Students ask one another questions each day.
   - Students write additional important ideas from the chapter in journals.

Relief map of the United States

1. Discuss map and map key.
2. Ask one another questions about the map. For example:
   - Show where the coastal plains are in the U.S.
   - How can you tell where mountains are on the map?
   - Where can plateaus be found?
3. Review and discuss other graphics from section 1.

Read aloud from Tom Sawyer.

Section 2: How Rivers Make Changes

1. Preview section 2: What do you think these pages will be about?
   - Look at headings.
   - Look at pictures and captions.

- Map of states with rivers—What do you already know about rivers in the U.S.?
2. Develop two or three questions that focus on the main ideas of the section.
3. Students write questions in journals.
4. Discuss possible answers.

Vocabulary

1. Write key vocabulary words and sentences in journals.
   - Draw a picture of a river and label parts: mouth, source, tributary, drainage basin, levee, dam, delta.
2. Look for clues in words.
3. Make word cards for key vocabulary terms.
4. Students add two or three words they did not know (after reading).
5. Use vocabulary word cards to review definitions.

Read

1. Day 1: Educational assistant reads to students, and they listen for main ideas.
   - Discuss answers to questions for journals.
   - Write answers for each question.
2. Day 2: Students read in pairs.
   - Students write main ideas in journals as questions.
   - Students ask one another questions each day.
   - Students write additional important ideas from section 2 in journals.

Map of United States with major rivers

1. Discuss mileage key and map.
   - Ask one another questions about the map. For example: Find the Mississippi. Where is the source of the Mississippi? Where is the mouth of the Mississippi? What body of water does the Mississippi empty into?
   - Find other major rivers of the United States.
   - How were rivers important to the development of the United States?
2. Use an elevation map.
   - Discuss what the map shows us.
   - Discuss use of map key.

Read aloud from **Tom Sawyer.**

Section 3: Climates in the United States

1. Preview section 3: What do you think these pages will be about?
   - Look at headings: What is a climate? How do climates differ in the U.S.?
   - Look at pictures and captions.
   - What does the temperature map tell us?
2. Develop two or three questions that focus on the main ideas of the section.
   - Students write questions in journals.
   - Discuss possible answers.

Vocabulary

1. Write key vocabulary words and sentences in journals.
   - Draw pictures where possible.
   - Look for clues in words.
2. Make word cards for key vocabulary terms.
   - Write definitions on the back of the cards.
3. Students add two or three words they did not know (after reading).
4. Use vocabulary word cards to review definitions.

Read

1. Day 1: Educational assistant reads to students, and they listen for main ideas.
   - Discuss answers to questions for journals.
   - Write answers for each question.
2. Day 2: Students read in pairs.
   - Students write main ideas in journals as questions.
   - Students ask one another questions each day.
   - Students write additional important ideas from section 3 in journals.

Maps of temperature differences in the United States

1. Discuss map keys and map contents.
   - Ask one another questions about the map. For example:
   - What temperature is represented by green in the key?
   - Where is the warmest/coldest place in January/July?
2. Discuss graphics from section 3 and what they tell us.

Read aloud from **Tom Sawyer.**

Section 4: Natural Resources

1. Preview section 4: What do you think these pages will be about?
   - Look at headings: What do you think natural resources are?
   - Look at pictures and captions.
2. Develop two or three questions that focus on the main ideas of the section.
3. Students write questions in journals.
4. Discuss possible answers.

Vocabulary

1. Write key vocabulary words and sentences in journals.
   - Draw pictures whenever possible.
   - Look for clues in words or think about similar words (synonyms).
2. Make word cards for key vocabulary terms.
   - Write definitions on the backs.
3. Students add two or three words they did not know (after reading).
4. Use vocabulary word cards to review definitions.

Read

1. Day 1: Educational assistant reads to students, and they listen for main ideas.
   - Discuss answers to questions for journals.
   - Write answers for each question in journals.
2. Day 2: Students read in pairs.
   - Students write main ideas in journals as questions.
   - Students ask one another questions each day.
   - Students write additional important ideas from section 4 in journals.
3. Discuss graphics in section 4 and what they tell us.

Map of natural resources in the United States

1. Ask one another questions about the map.
2. Students make observations from map. For example:
   - Wisconsin has many farming resources.

Read aloud from **Tom Sawyer.**

C

EL CLUB DE LECTURA/THE READING CLUB: FIFTH-GRADE SOCIAL STUDIES

El Club de Lectura/The Reading Club may be used in fourth and fifth grades only with significant modifications. At these grade levels the content area requirements have become much more extensive. Therefore, as we experimented with a design for El Club de Lectura at Hayes Bilingual School, it became very clear that one of the subject areas should be used as the focus. We opted to design the program around social studies at both grade levels.

The teachers at each grade level determined the focus areas to be developed during these lessons. These areas were selected in relation to the Wisconsin State Reading and Social Studies Standards. The fifth-grade teachers wanted their students to be able to identify main ideas, use graphic organizers, and compare/contrast ideas but also wanted their students to focus on activation of prior knowledge, expository writing, and portfolio development.

The social studies series being used at Hayes Bilingual School lent itself well to this purpose. There was an emphasis on developing thinking skills and social studies reading skills and strategies already present in the series. The goal was to have students learn these skills and strategies to strengthen both their reading and their social studies abilities.

Although the format was quite repetitive, students began to look forward to these sessions. Having the educational assistant read the passages to the students first enabled them to concentrate on the content without having to struggle with reading the text also. Additional activities provided them with opportunities to solidify their understanding of content and vocabulary. Discussing responses orally first enabled students to develop better understanding of concepts before they were required to write them. A trade book was also selected as a read-aloud at each grade level. The book selected further expanded the topic under study in the social studies text.

It took a few weeks before students had built a base for reading and understanding the social studies text. But once they had developed some background in both areas, they began to move along at a faster rate. As much as possible, the Club de Lectura groups at these grade levels paralleled what the teachers were teaching in social studies with the rest of the class.

While this class was taught completely in Spanish, the plans are described in English to enable all to get the gist of this approach.

Focus Areas

- Activation of prior knowledge
- Graphic organizers
- Main idea
- Compare/contrast
- Expository writing
- Portfolio development

Materials Needed

- Journal for each student
- Word cards (index cards)

CHAPTER I

The focus here is on main ideas (graphic organizers).

Section 1: Cities of the Industrial Revolution

1. Preview section 1: What do you think these pages will be about?

- Look at headings.
- Look at pictures and captions.
- Look at end of section questions.
- Look at charts.
- Look at maps.
- What do you already know about this topic?

2. Develop three or four questions that focus on the main ideas of section 1.
   - Students write questions in journals.
   - Discuss possible answers.

Vocabulary

1. Write key vocabulary words (often in highlighted print) on cards.
   - Write word part meanings and definition phrases on front.
   - On the back of the card, write a sentence or two from the text using the word.
   - Draw pictures when possible.
2. Students add two or three word cards for words they did not know (after reading).
3. Use vocabulary word cards to review definitions.

Read

1. Day 1: Educational assistant reads to students, and they listen for main ideas.
   - Discuss answers to questions for journals.
   - Write answers for each question.
2. Day 2: Students read in pairs.
   - Students write main ideas in journals as questions. For example: Can you name some important inventions from the 1880s? What is a monopoly? Who was a person who became rich from steel?
   - Students ask one another questions each day.

Graphic organizer

1. Students use a T-chart to outline main ideas and supporting details from the section.

Graphics

1. Students ask one another questions using information from the graph.

Read aloud from book about immigration in the 1880s

Expository writing

1. Write about one invention from this era and how it changed people's lives.

Section 2: Problems Cities Faced

1. Preview section 2: What do you think these pages will be about?
   - Look at headings.
   - Look at pictures and captions: Are there some similarities to today?
   - Look at charts.
   - What do you already know about this topic?
2. Develop three or four questions that focus on the main ideas of section 1.
   - Students write questions in journals.
   - Discuss possible answers.

Vocabulary

1. Write key vocabulary words on cards.
   - Write word part meanings and definition phrases on front.
   - Write a sentence or two from the text using the word on back.
   - Draw pictures when possible.
2. Students add two or three words they did not know (after reading).
   - Use vocabulary word cards to review definitions.

Read

1. Day 1: Educational assistant reads to students, and they listen for main ideas.
   - Discuss answers to questions for journals.
   - Write answers for each question.
2. Day 2: Students read in pairs.
   - Students write main ideas in journals as questions.
   - Students ask one another questions each day.

Graphic organizer

1. Students use a cause and effect chart to highlight problems cities faced in the late 1800s and early 1900s.

Graphs and charts

1. Students determine what graphics from the section tell us and make statements using information from the graphics.

Expository writing

1. Students write a brief report based on the graphics studied in the section above.

Read aloud from book about immigration in the 1880s.

Section 3: Immigration

1. Preview section 3: What do you think these pages will be about?
   - Look at headings.
   - Look at pictures and captions.
   - Look at maps and graph.
   - What do you already know about this topic? How is it similar to today?
2. Develop three or four questions that focus on the main ideas of section 1.
   - Students write questions in journals.
   - Discuss possible answers.

Vocabulary

1. Write key vocabulary words on cards.
   - Write word part meanings and definition phrases on front.
   - Write a sentence or two from the text using the word on back.
   - Draw pictures when possible.
2. Students add two or three words they did not know (after reading).
3. Use vocabulary word cards to review definitions.

Read

1. Day 1: Educational assistant reads to students, and they listen for main ideas.
   - Discuss answers to questions for journals.
   - Write answers for each question in journals.
2. Day 2: Students read in pairs.
   - Students write main ideas in journals as questions.
   - Students ask one another questions each day.
   - Students create a chart to show where immigrants were coming from between 1880 and 1910.

Map of world

1. Label a map of the world to show where immigrants were coming from during this era.

2. Create a graphic to show how immigrants were treated or create a graphic to compare and contrast immigrants from 1900 and 2000.

Graphs

1. Review and interpret graphics from this section.
2. Students ask one another questions using information in graph.

Expository writing

1. Students write a journal entry as if they were a child entering the United States as an immigrant in 1900.

Read aloud from book about immigration in the 1880s.

1. Compare immigration today to immigration 100 years ago.
   - Where did people come from in each era?
   - Why did people come?
   - What was life like in each era?

Section 4: The Growth of Large Cities

1. Preview section 4: What do you think the section will be about?
   - Look at headings.
   - Look at pictures and captions.
2. Develop three or four questions that focus on the main ideas of section 4.
   - Students write questions in journals.
   - Discuss possible answers.

Vocabulary

1. Write key vocabulary words on cards.
   - Write word part meanings and definition phrases on front.
   - Write a sentence or two from the text using the word on back.
   - Draw pictures when possible.
   - Look for clues in words and similar words.
2. Students add two or three words they did not know (after reading).
3. Use vocabulary word cards to review definitions.

Read

1. Day 1: Educational assistant reads to students, and they listen for main ideas.
   - Discuss ideas for each question.
   - Write answers to each question in journal.

2. Day 2: Students read in pairs.
   - Students write main ideas in journals as questions.
   - Students ask one another questions each day.

Graphic organizer

1. Students create a graphic to outline additional important ideas from section 4.

Expository writing

1. Students write a journal entry comparing cities from 1900 and 2000.

Read aloud from book about immigration in the 1880s.

Portfolios

1. Choose two social studies items for your portfolio.
2. Answer these questions:
   - Why did you include these items?
   - What do they show about what you understand in social studies?
   - What did you do well in each item?
   - What did you learn from doing this assignment?
   - What goals do you want to set for yourself in social studies?

STUDENT PORTFOLIO REFLECTION

Name: _____ Date: _____

Write a brief description of the two social studies items you selected for your portfolio.

1.

2.

Answer the following questions:

• Why did you include these items?

• What do they show about what you understand in social studies?

• What did you do well in each item?

• What did you learn from doing this assignment?

• What goals do you want to set for yourself in social studies?

D

SCREENING MATERIALS IN ENGLISH AND SPANISH

Name:_____ Date: _____

Uppercase Letters   Lowercase Letters

Fall	Winter	Spring	Fall	Winter	Spring
A	A	A	a	a	a
P	P	P	p	p	p
T	T	T	t	t	t
V	V	V	v	v	v
K	K	K	k	k	k
D	D	D	d	d	d
F	F	F	f	f	f
H	H	H	h	h	h
I	I	I	i	i	i
M	M	M	m	m	m
Z	Z	Z	z	z	z
B	B	B	b	b	b
J	J	J	j	j	j
Q	Q	Q	q	q	q
S	S	S	s	s	s
Y	Y	Y	y	y	y
X	X	X	x	x	x
N	N	N	n	n	n
C	C	C	c	c	c
U	U	U	u	u	u
E	E	E	e	e	e
R	R	R	r	r	r
L	L	L	l	l	l
W	W	W	w	w	w
O	O	O	o	o	o
G	G	G	g	g	g

Comments:

LETTERS OF THE ALPHABET

A P T V K D

F H I M Z B

J Q S Y X N

C U E R L W

O G

---

a p t v k d f

h i m z b j q

s y x n c u e

r l w o g

Name: _____ Date: _____

Graded Word Lists

Preprimer	**Sight**	**Analysis**	**Primer**	**Sight**	**Analysis**
little	____	____	good	____	____
blue	____	____	ride	____	____
you	____	____	are	____	____
and	____	____	they	____	____
three	____	____	like	____	____
it	____	____	want	____	____
play	____	____	at	____	____
up	____	____	pretty	____	____
come	____	____	but	____	____
funny	____	____	she	____	____
big	____	____	with	____	____
me	____	____	eat	____	____
run	____	____	please	____	____
yellow	____	____	black	____	____
see	____	____	came	____	____
jump	____	____	he	____	____
go	____	____	ran	____	____
down	____	____	new	____	____
the	____	____	out	____	____
red	____	____	do	____	____

Number Correct: _____   Number Correct: _____

Scoring Guide for Graded Word Lists		
Independent	Instructional	Frustration
20, 19	18, 17, 16, 15, 14	13 or less

Name: _____ Date: _____

Graded Word Lists

Grade 1	Sight	Analysis	Grade 2	Sight	Analysis
from	____	____	why	____	____
when	____	____	found	____	____
live	____	____	sing	____	____
after	____	____	always	____	____
some	____	____	which	____	____
open	____	____	made	____	____
thank	____	____	does	____	____
could	____	____	been	____	____
old	____	____	write	____	____
any	____	____	upon	____	____
walk	____	____	pull	____	____
take	____	____	fast	____	____
put	____	____	because	____	____
know	____	____	would	____	____
fly	____	____	sleep	____	____
over	____	____	don't	____	____
ask	____	____	read	____	____
her	____	____	first	____	____
stop	____	____	right	____	____
them	____	____	their	____	____

Number Correct: _____   Number Correct: _____

Scoring Guide for Graded Word Lists		
Independent	Instructional	Frustration
20, 19	18, 17, 16, 15, 14	13 or less

Name: _____ Date: _____

Graded Word Lists

Grade 3	Sight	Analysis	Grade 4*	Sight	Analysis
draw	____	____	bike	____	____
keep	____	____	castle	____	____
warm	____	____	jungle	____	____
bring	____	____	bullet	____	____
today	____	____	factory	____	____
eight	____	____	stripe	____	____
try	____	____	problem	____	____
grow	____	____	target	____	____
about	____	____	capture	____	____
laugh	____	____	sleeve	____	____
show	____	____	pump	____	____
far	____	____	sausage	____	____
clean	____	____	electric	____	____
never	____	____	business	____	____
start	____	____	instant	____	____
better	____	____	balance	____	____
hold	____	____	surround	____	____
carry	____	____	invention	____	____
much	____	____	accident	____	____
small	____	____	rifle	____	____

Number Correct: _____   Number Correct: _____

Scoring Guide for Graded Word Lists		
Independent	Instructional	Frustration
20, 19	18, 17, 16, 15, 14	13 or less

* from the *Jerry Johns informal reading inventory: Early literacy assessments and teaching strategies*, Dubuque, IA: Kendall/Hunt.

SAMPLE READING MISCUE EVALUATION FORM

Name: _____ Date: _____

Lunch

Today I went shopping with my mother.

We bought some bread.

We bought some peanut butter.

We bought some jelly.

We bought some milk and apples.

Then we went home and made a nice lunch.

Miscue Analysis

In this format, the examiner marks a check above each word read correctly. Errors are noted where they occur in the text.

Comprehension of story

The student was:
_____ able to accurately retell the story (2 points)
_____ able to accurately retell some of the story (1 points)
_____ unable to retell the story/inaccurately retold the story (0 point)

Comprehension Score: _____

Analysis of Reading (check all that apply)

Did the student:

____ read the story accurately and fluently
____ use pictures to help figure out the words
____ sound out words
____ read the story accurately but very hesitantly and slowly
____ look only at the pictures and make up the story
____ not know what to do when he/she came to an unknown word

Name:
Grade Level:
Date:

Nombre:_____ Fecha: _____

Letras Mayúsculas   Letras Minúsculas

otoño	invierno	primavera	otoño	invierno	primavera
A	A	A	a	a	a
P	P	P	p	p	p
T	T	T	t	t	t
V	V	V	v	v	v
K	K	K	k	k	k
D	D	D	d	d	d
Ñ	Ñ	Ñ	ñ	ñ	ñ
F	F	F	f	f	f
H	H	H	h	h	h
I	I	I	i	i	i
M	M	M	m	m	m
Z	Z	Z	z	z	z
B	B	B	b	b	b
J	J	J	j	j	j
Q	Q	Q	q	q	q
S	S	S	s	s	s
Y	Y	Y	y	y	y
X	X	X	x	x	x
N	N	N	n	n	n
Ll	Ll	Ll	ll	ll	ll
C	C	C	c	c	c
U	U	U	u	u	u
E	E	E	e	e	e
R	R	R	r	r	r
L	L	L	l	l	l
W	W	W	w	w	w
O	O	O	o	o	o
G	G	G	g	g	g

Comentarios:

EL ABECEDARIO

A P T V K D Ñ

F H I M Z B J

Q S Y X N Ll C

U E R L W O G

---

a p t v k d ñ

f h i m z b j

q s y x n ll c

u e r l w o g

Comentarios:

Nombre: _____ Fecha: _____

Graded Word Lists

Nivel PP	Sight	Analysis	Nivel 1.1	Sight	Analysis
oso	____	____	familia	____	____
no	____	____	ver	____	____
jugar	____	____	correr	____	____
vamos	____	____	buscar	____	____
yo	____	____	y	____	____
tomar	____	____	gordo	____	____
voy	____	____	mucho	____	____
ser	____	____	tengo	____	____
grande	____	____	bien	____	____
los	____	____	vivir	____	____
saltar	____	____	es	____	____
mirar	____	____	dar	____	____
todo	____	____	van	____	____
gustar	____	____	ir	____	____
mi	____	____	sentar	____	____
decir	____	____	hay	____	____
en	____	____	saber	____	____
ahora	____	____	así	____	____
otro	____	____	mirar	____	____
decir	____	____	oír	____	____

Número Correcto: _____   Número Correcto: _____

Scoring Guide for Graded Word Lists		
Independent	Instructional	Frustration
20, 19	18, 17, 16, 15, 14	13 or less

Nombre: _____ Fecha: _____

Graded Word Lists

Nivel 1.2	Sight	Analysis	Nivel 2	Sight	Analysis
ir	___	___	porque	___	___
también	___	___	poco	___	___
allí	___	___	alguno	___	___
donde	___	___	antes	___	___
pensar	___	___	sorpresas	___	___
oír	___	___	entrar	___	___
cuando	___	___	deber	___	___
salir	___	___	escuela	___	___
muy	___	___	llevar	___	___
vivir	___	___	también	___	___
hay	___	___	señor	___	___
yo	___	___	ayudar	___	___
rojo	___	___	sé	___	___
poner	___	___	quién	___	___
subir	___	___	ardilla	___	___
llevar	___	___	cumpleaños	___	___
por	___	___	bosque	___	___
venir	___	___	timbre	___	___
son	___	___	estrella	___	___
pequeño	___	___	calle	___	___

Número Correcto: _____   Número Correcto: _____

Scoring Guide for Graded Word Lists		
Independent	Instructional	Frustration
20, 19	18, 17, 16, 15, 14	13 or less

Nombre: _____ Fecha: _____

Form A: Graded Word Lists

Nivel 2.2	Sight	Analysis	Nivel 3.1	Sight	Analysis
aburría	____	____	aguda	____	____
comenzó	____	____	agujas	____	____
contarles	____	____	aseaba	____	____
contentos	____	____	brillantes	____	____
descansar	____	____	campanilla	____	____
empezó	____	____	corriente	____	____
entonces	____	____	cumpleaños	____	____
guerras	____	____	despertador	____	____
historias	____	____	exactamente	____	____
hombrecillo	____	____	levantarse	____	____
miserias	____	____	manejarlo	____	____
periódico	____	____	numeritos	____	____
primavera	____	____	prepararse	____	____
rompecabezas	____	____	temprano	____	____
sentaron	____	____	útil	____	____

Número Correcto: _____   Número Correcto: _____

Scoring Guide for Graded Word Lists		
Independent	Instructional	Frustration
15, 14	13, 12, 11	10 or less

Nombre: _____ Fecha: _____

Form A: Graded Word Lists

Nivel 3.2	Sight	Analysis	Nivel 4.1	Sight	Analysis
abonaban	____	____	agarrarse	____	____
alimentada	____	____	asombrada	____	____
cántaro	____	____	avanzado	____	____
criaban	____	____	confiada	____	____
fermentos	____	____	disparatados	____	____
herbían	____	____	dispuestos	____	____
incorporaba	____	____	enseguida	____	____
necesarios	____	____	equivocaba	____	____
ordenaba	____	____	hubieran	____	____
orear	____	____	marineros	____	____
prado	____	____	martillar	____	____
producía	____	____	navegante	____	____
utilizarían	____	____	pichones	____	____
rompecabezas	____	____	plumón	____	____
hierba	____	____	proyectos	____	____

Número Correcto: _____   Número Correcto: _____

Scoring Guide for Graded Word Lists		
Independent	Instructional	Frustration
15, 14	13, 12, 11	10 or less

UNA MUESTRA DE UN FORMULARIO PARA EVALUAR LA LECTURA

Nombre: _____ Fecha: _____

La Merienda

Fui de compras con mi mamá.

Compramos pan.

Compramos jamón.

Compramos dos manzanas.

Compramos leche.

Y compramos unas galletas.

Entonces fuimos al parque para una merienda.

Comprehensión del cuento

Hacer un resumen:
_____ Se puede relatar el cuento exactamente (2)
_____ Se puede relatar unas partes del cuento (1)
_____ No se puede relatar ningunas partes del cuento (0)

Calificación: _____

Análisis de Lectura

Título del libro:
Nivel:
Serie:

_____ leyó el cuento con facilidad y fluidez
_____ leyó el cuento en una manera precisa pero muy despacio
_____ usó las láminas como una ayuda en leer
_____ usó las láminas para crear su propio cuento
_____ usó la fonética como una ayuda en leer
_____ no empleo ningunas estrategias para ayudar con palabras desconocidas

E

WORD WORKS MATERIALS

The purpose of the Word Works component of The Reading Club is to help children 1) learn the letters of the alphabet and the sounds they represent, 2) understand sound and letter patterns within words, and 3) apply what they learn in the Word Works component to their everyday reading and writing activities.

ENGLISH

In English, three formats are recommended for the development of facility with word formation: Making Words, onset and rime, and vowel/consonant patterns.

Making Words

Patricia Cunningham (1995) has developed a very effective format for exploring letters, sounds, word parts, and words within words. Consult her text and the text of Cunningham et al. (2000) for additional ideas regarding Making Words and study of prefixes and suffixes. Some samples from Making Words are included below. In this format children are given letters in random order that will make up a word (for example, *candy*). The children are asked to name each letter and then form smaller words that can be found in the word *candy*, for example *an, Dan, can, day*. Then they are asked to use all of the letters to form a single word, *candy*. Several sound and letter patterns can be explored in this fashion. For example, they might be asked to note rhyming words, long and short vowel patterns, or form two words with the same letters (for example, *art* and *tar*).

As suggested in chapter 2, the students should begin by using individual letter cards or magnetic letters in forming the words. Once children know their letters and sounds very well and can form new words quite easily, the word cards or magnetic letters can be substituted for writing words in their writing booklets. For example, children can be told that they will be forming a seven-letter word. They would make seven dashes on their paper and then work at spelling the word. In any format, the final word should be reviewed with the group to enable them to check their work. As they gain more understanding of how words are formed, they may begin to note their own patterns. Patterns that are studied in this component of The Reading Club are only valuable when students can transfer what they learn to their reading and writing activities. Care should be taken to help students make that transfer.

Onset and Rime (Word Families)

Onset and rime refers to what was traditionally called work with "word families." The rime is the main portion of the word, and the onset is the initial sound(s). For example, if the rime is *–in*, the onsets might be *f, p, w, sh*. When the onset and rime components are put together, children may form the words *fin, pin, win*, and *shin*. It is recommended that educational assistants alternate between Making Words (Cunningham, 1995) and the onset and rime activities to give students more flexibility in understanding how words are formed.

As the children improve in their ability to manipulate sounds and word parts, more complex words might be added. However, the level of the activities should always remain at the instructional level of the students. Selecting words that take more than four or five class sessions for students to master are probably too difficult and should be modified to match the students' comfort level in learning about words.

In this format, children are given a sheet that contains a box at the top of the page for vowels and a second box for consonants. They are given two or three vowels and about five consonants and asked to form their own words on the lines provided. The boxes at the top of the page might also be substituted for onset and rime combinations.

SPANISH

Spanish is a very phonetic language and can be explored best by emergent readers through the use of syllables. In Spanish, children hear vowel sounds more readily than consonants (in English, consonant sounds are more apparent to emergent readers); therefore, introducing the vowel sounds initially and then adding new consonants one at a time makes phonics learning much more manageable for students beginning their reading instruction in Spanish. As mentioned in chapter 2, the Spanish Word Works represents a controlled vocabulary approach, in that only letters that have been previously introduced and practiced are used in conjunction with the new consonant/sound being introduced. A suggested sequence of Word Works is presented below.

WORD WORKS

(from Cunningham, P., 1995. *Phonics they use: Words for reading and writing*, 2nd ed., New York: HarperCollins)

First and second grades

1. candy:	a , an, Dan, can, and, day, candy
2. plant:	ant, tan, pan, nap, tap, pant, plant
3. brake:	are, bar, bear, rake, bake, brake
4. crane:	an, ran, can, car, near, cane, crane
5. shave:	he, she, has, have, save, vase, shave
6. spends:	pen, den, send, pens, spends
7. spent:	ten, pen, pens, sent, spent
8. when:	we, he, hen, new, when
9. peach:	he, cap, each, cheap, peach
10. wheat:	hat, wet, the, then, what, net, eat, wheat
11. pumpkin:	pin, pup, pump, snip, pumpkin
12. balloon:	ball, nab, tab, loon, balloon
13. fastest:	fat, fate, sets, fast, test, ate, state, fastest
14. notebook:	boot, book, took, note, tone, notebook
15. sandbox:	and, sand, box, band, bond, sandbox

ONSET AND RIME PATTERNS

Onset	Rime	Onset	Rime
b, d, h, l, p, s	*-ad*	c, D, g, s, w	*-ave*
c, D, f, m, p, r, t, v	*-an*	c, b, l, m, r, t, w	*-ake*
b, l, r, s, t, w	*-ag*	c, f, g, n, s, t	*-ame*
b, c, f, h, m, p, r, s	*-at*	d, g, h, l, m, r	*-ate*
b, f, l, N, r, T	*-ed*	b, h, n, s, tr	*-eat*
B, d, h, m, p, t	*-en*	b, j, k, p, w	*-eep*
b, j, l, m, n, p, s, w	*-et*	f, n, s, w, gr, bl	*-eed*
b, n, p, r, t, v, w	*-est*	b, p, r, t, pr	*-each*
B, f, h, J, p, w, st	*-ill*	f, m, p, t, N	*-ile*
b, d, p, w, f, tw	*-ig*	d, f, l, m, n, p, v, wh	*-ine*
f, p, t, w, gr, sh	*-in*	d, dr, f, h, l	*-ive*
d, h, k, l, sl	*-id*	h, s, w, gl, br, pr, sl	*-ide*
d, f, h, j, l, fr	*-og*	b, c, f, g, s, t	*-old*
c, h, m, t, dr, cr, st	*-op*	c, p, w, br	*-oke*
B, c, j, r, bl	*-ob*	b, c, ph, t, st	*-one*
b, c, h, l, t, br, cr	*-ook*		
b, d, l, t, tr, st, cl	*-uck*	J, t	*-une*
c, h, r, s, t, cl, st	*-ub*	m	*-ule*
b, d, h, m, r, t, shr	*-ug*		

FORMANDO PALABRAS

Mm	ma, me, mi, mo, mu (Mamá, Memo, Mimí, ama, mima, mía)
Tt	ta, te, ti, to, tu (tío, tía, mato, tomate)
Cc	ca, co, cu (cama, coco, Cuca, como, cometa)
Nn	na, ne, ni, no, un (nena, cuna, mano, Anita, tiene, camino)
Pp	pa, pe, pi, po, pu (pipa, papá, tapa, Pepe, pan)
Ss	sa, se, si, so, su (sapo, oso, suma, sopa, saco, cose, Susana)
Qq	que, qui (queso, quema, Quico, quita, paquete, máquina)
Bb	ba, be, bi, bo, bu (bata, cubo, beso, botas, cubeta, buenas, bonita)
Dd	da, de, di, do, du (dedo, dado, nudo, nada, dudo, nido)
Rr	ra, re, ri, ro, ru (rosas, ratón, ropa, ruta, risa, Rosita, mariposa)
Gg	ga, go, gu (gota, goma, amigo, gato, gusano, ganado)
Ll	la, le, li, lo, lu (lobo, luna, león, Lola, lista, pela)
Ch	cha, che, chi, cho, chu (coche, ocho, leche, noche, lechuga, chocolate)
Vv	va, ve, vi, vo, vu (vaso, vela, venado, nieve, vaca, Valentín)
Ll, ll	lla, lle, lli, llo, llu (silla, caballo, anillo, gallina, llave, llego)
Gg	ge, gi (gitano, gelatina, gemelos, vigila)
Cc	ce, ci (cocina, doce, cebolla, racimo, Cecilia, tocino)
Rr	rra, rre, rri, rro, rru (carreta, torre, burro, parrillo, corre, barro, perro)
Ññ	ña, ñe, ñi, ño, ñu (piña, uña, araña, muñeca, año, piñata)
Jj	ja, je, ji, jo, ju (ojo, abeja, conejo, dibujo, Juan, pájaro)
Ff	fa, fe, fi, fo, fu (foca, foto, sofá, teléfono, fila, Felipe, café)
Zz	za, ze, zi, zo, zu (zapato, taza, zorro, cabeza, azul, lazo)
Yy	ya, ye, yi, yo, yu (yoyo, rayo, yema, mayo, payaso, arroyo, ayudo)
Gg	gue, gui (guitarra, águila, amiguito, juguete)
Gg	güe, güi (yegüita, cigüeña, pingüino, bilingüe)
Xx	xa, xe, xi, xo, xu (México, sexto, Calixto, examen, éxito, saxofón, Félix)
Hh	ha, he, hi, ho, hu (helado, búho, hielo, harina, hermano, hormigas, horno)
Kk	ka, ke, ki, ko, ku (kilo, kimono, koala, karate, kiosco)
Ww	wa, we, w, wo, wu (Wendy, waffle)
tr	tra, tre, tri, tro, tru (sastre, trece, Trini, trigo, tren, travieso)

br   bra, bre, bri, bro, bru (cabrito, brujo, brincando, cabritos, pobres, libritos)

pr   pra, pre, pri, pro, pru (primo, sorpresa, prudente, pradera, compra, preciosos)

cr   cra, cre, cri, cro, cru (crema, recreo, escritura, cristal, crecer)

dr   dra, dre, dri, dro, dru (madre, piedra, cuadro, golondrina, ladrillo, Pedrito)

gr   gra, gre, gri, gro, gru (grupo, negro, grillo, fotógrafo, alegre, regreso)

fr   fra, fre, fri, fro, fru (Alfredo, Africa, frutero, fruta, fresca, disfrutamos)

bl   bla, ble, bli, blo, blu (blusa, niebla, público, problema, pueblo, amable, mueble)

fl   fla, fle, fli, flo, flu (flecha, florero, flauta, reflejos, flaco, rifle)

gl   gla, gle, gli, glo, glu (Gloria, iglesia, gladiola, arregla, globo)

cl   cla, cle, cli, clo, clu (clima, clases, chicle, clave, conclusión, Claudia)

pl   pla, ple, pli, plo, plu (playa, plátano, pluma, simple, aplicado, plantas)

F

STUDENT MONITORING FORMS

WRITING RULES

Name: _____ Date: _____

1. Do not start any sentences with:
    - small letters
    - but
    - and
2. Do not repeat. Start each sentence differently. Not:
    - I like my mom.
    - I like my dad.
    - I like my grandma.

    But rather:
    - I love my Mom.
    - We go shopping together.
    - She buys me very nice clothes.
3. Finish each sentence with a period. Count your periods.
4. Write only one *and* for each sentence.
5. Follow these steps:
    - write
    - read
    - fix
    - read again
    - fix again

REGLAS DE ESCRITURA

Nombre: _____   Fecha: _____

1. Nunca empieces con:
   - Letra mínuscula
   - pero
   - y
2. No repetir la misma oración. Empieza cada oración diferente. No:
   - Yo limpiaré.
   - Yo comeré toda la comida.
   - Yo iré al . . .

   Sí:
   - Voy a ayudar a mi mamá con . . .
   - En la cena tendremos . . .
   - Después de la cena mi papá me llevará al …
3. Toda oración lleva punto final.
4. No repitas la palabra "y" más de una vez en la oración.
5. Sigue estos pasos:
   - escribe
   - lee
   - corrige
   - lee otra vez
   - corrige otra vez

SELF-ASSESSMENT

Name: _____ Date: _____

Reading Fluency

_____ My reading is very smooth and easy for a listener to follow. (3)

_____ My reading is fairly smooth and fairly easy for a listener to follow. (2)

_____ My reading is not too smooth and not too easy for a listener to follow. (1)

Story Retelling

Part 1:

_____ In my retelling I included all of the important information. (3)

_____ In my retelling I included some of the important information. (2)

_____ In my retelling I included only a little of the important information. (1)

Part 2:

_____ In my retelling I included none of the unimportant details. (3)

_____ In my retelling I included some of the unimportant details. (2)

_____ In my retelling I included lots of unimportant details. (1)

ASSESSING MY READING

Name: _____   Date: _____

Easy books I can read:

    1.
    2.
    3.

A book that I'm trying to read better:

Strategies that I use:

    1. Look at the picture.
    2. Think about what would make sense.
    3. Get my mouth ready to read the word.
    4. Skip the word and keep reading.
    5. Think about what I already know about this.

How do I feel about myself as a reader?

_____ very good
_____ ok
_____ not so good

EVALUANDO LA LECTURA

Nombre: _____ Fecha: _____

Libros sencillos que puedo leer:

   1.
   2.
   3.

Libro que quiero dominar:

Estrategias que uso:

   1. Mirar el dibujo.
   2. Pensar en algo que tenga sentido.
   3. Volver a leer con la boca en posición de leer.
   4. Saltar la palabra y continuar leyendo.
   5. Buscar por porciones que ya conozco.

¿Cómo te sentiste como lector?

_____ muy bien
_____ así, así
_____ no muy bueno

READING CLUB WRITING RUBRIC: SELF-ASSESSMENT

Name: _____   Date: _____

Three Points

_____ All of my sentences begin with a capital letter.
_____ Each of my sentences begin with a different word.
_____ All of my sentences end with a period (.) or a question mark (?).
_____ My writing is very interesting.
_____ My writing is about one topic.

Two Points

_____ Some of my sentences begin with a capital letter.
_____ Some of my sentences begin with a different word.
_____ Some of my sentences end with a period (.) or a question mark (?).
_____ My writing is somewhat interesting.
_____ Most of my writing is about one topic.

One Point

_____ None of my sentences begin with a capital letter.
_____ None of my sentences begin with a different word.
_____ None of my sentences end with a period (.) or a question mark (?).
_____ My writing is not interesting.
_____ My writing is about too many topics.

Check off the steps you followed in your writing:
- write
- read
- fix
- read again
- fix again

READING CLUB WRITING RUBRIC: PEER ASSESSMENT

Name: _____ Date: _____

Three Points

_____ All of the sentences begin with a capital letter.
_____ Each sentence begins with a different word.
_____ All of the sentences end with a period (.) or a question mark (?).
_____ The writing is very interesting.
_____ The writing is about one topic.

Two Points

_____ Some of the sentences begin with a capital letter.
_____ Some of the sentences begin with a different word.
_____ Some of the sentences end with a period (.) or a question mark (?).
_____ The writing is somewhat interesting.
_____ Most of the writing is about one topic.

One Point

_____ None of the sentences begin with a capital letter.
_____ None of the sentences begin with a different word.
_____ None of the sentences end with a period (.) or a question mark (?).
_____ The writing is not interesting.
_____ The writing is about too many topics.

INDIVIDUAL READING LOG

Name: _____ School Year: _____

1. Title: _____

Author: _____ Date: _____

2. Title: _____

Author: _____ Date: _____

3. Title: _____

Author: _____ Date: _____

4. Title: _____

Author: _____ Date: _____

5. Title: _____

Author: _____ Date: _____

6. Title: _____

Author: _____ Date: _____

7. Title: _____

Author: _____ Date: _____

8. Title: _____

Author: _____ Date: _____

9. Title: _____

Author: _____ Date: _____

10. Title: _____

Author: _____ Date: _____

11. Title: _____

Author: _____ Date: _____

Ⓖ

THE READING CLUB/EL CLUB DE LECTURA INSERVICE PLANS

INSERVICE SESSION 1: OVERVIEW OF THE READING CLUB PLAN

Overview of Rationale
   Struggling students
   Acceleration
   Goal: Catch students up to peers
      Small groups
      Integration of language arts
      Active learning
      Individualized instruction
Usually: teacher + reading specialist
   Here: reading specialist + teacher + educational assistants
      Educational assistants to take lead
      Second grade: 45-minute sessions with four students
      First grade: 30-minute sessions with two to four students each
Role of metacognition: Development of reading/writing strategies
   Reading
      Predicting
      Picture clues

Retelling
Context clues
Writing
Single topic (Don't specify number of sentences)
Making words
Letter recognition
Sound/symbol relationship

INSERVICE SESSION 2: OVERVIEW OF THE READING CLUB LESSON

Overview of Lesson
Introducing new book
Echo/choral reading
Introduce students to new strategies
Use of reading strategies
Rereading familiar books
Strengthen story structure
Develop sight word vocabulary
Build confidence
Stress articulation of use of strategies
Word Works
Develop facility with "features" of words
Build sight word vocabulary
Writing sample and sharing
Connect making words and reading
Develop confidence in self as reader/writer
Student assessment/self-assessment
Students and educational assistants assess progress
This week I worked on _____.
This is how I did _____.
Kid-watching
Students set goals
Next week I want to _____.

INSERVICE SESSION 3: OVERVIEW OF THE READING CLUB SCREENING

Determine process for pre/post testing
    Letter recognition
    Word lists
    Miscue analysis
    Writing sample
    Dictation
Scheduling
    Initial screening
        Student selection
        Establishing a screening schedule
    Establishing a lesson schedule for each group of students
    Schedule for coordinator to visit
Selection of trade books
Miscue analysis sample
    Omission
    Substitution
"To do" list
    Word Works materials
    Booklets for each child
        Word Works section
        Writing section
        Assessment section
    Assessing student progress
        Screening materials
            Alphabet (teacher and student sheets)
        Writing sample
            Sheet to be included in booklet
        Miscue analysis
            Text
            Recording sheet
        Dictation
        Writing sample

INSERVICE SESSION 4: READING AND WRITING

1. Reading readiness vs. emergent literacy
   Focus on skill development vs. development of meaning
2. Reading and writing stages
   Present stages of reading: discuss students' reading stages
   Present stages of writing: educational assistants
       examine samples of students' writing.
       place students on the reading/writing continuum.
3. Inform parents of membership in The Reading Club/El Club de Lectura

See sample letters.

Invite to lessons.

Share information with classroom teacher for parent-teacher conferences.

Letters to parents

Apreciados padres/encargados:

Esta carta es para infórmales que su hijo/a_____
ha sido escojido para estar en un programa de intervención de lectura.
Dicho programa ayuda a los estudiantes a mejorar su desarrollo en las
destrezas de lectura y escritura. El grupo no tiene más de cuatro estudiantes así que obtiene más atención de uno a uno. Esto se lleva a cabo
todos los días; por eso, es importante que su hijo/a este en la escuela.

    Este programa de lectura es enseñado por asistentes de maestros
paraprofesionales aquí en la Escuela _____. La ayudante
que trabaja con su hijo/a es _____.

    Cualquier día que usted desee hablar con dicha ayudante de maestro
o llegarse a la escuela para observar en el salón, están más que bien-
venidos para hacerlo.

    La hora en que su hijo/a está en el grupo de lectura es a las _____
y será en el salón _____.

Sinceramente,

Dear Parents:

This letter is to inform you that your son/daughter, _____,
has been selected to participate in a reading intervention program. This
program helps the student to better develop his or her reading and writing skills. The small group has no more than four students, therefore,
the child receives more one-on-one attention. It is taught every day, so
it is very important that your child be at school.

The reading program is taught by trained paraprofessional assistants
here at _____ School. The assistant who works with your
child is _____.

Anytime you wish to speak to that assistant or come and watch your
child in the class, you are more than welcome.

Your child's class time is at _____ in Room _____.

Sincerely,

INSERVICE SESSION 5: STRATEGY DEVELOPMENT

1. Introduction to reading strategies
   Providing opportunities for students to learn and practice strate-
   gies
      Picture clues
         Use sample books
         Have educational assistant practice teaching use of picture
         clues
      Context clues
         Ask children, "Does this make sense?" (use clues in sentence)
         Have educational assistant practice teaching use of picture clues
      Prediction
         Link to own life
         Reread for clues
   Determine strategy to focus on for the week
   Monitor progress and discuss at next inservice session

2. Discuss next steps in each area
   Reading
   Writing
   Word Works
3. Discuss rotating children in and out of The Reading Club
   Solid grade-level proficiency
   No more than four per group
4. Determine areas to focus on for next week

INSERVICE SESSION 6: END-OF-YEAR CELEBRATION

Sample Agenda

El Club de Lectura
End-of-Year Celebration
June 1, 2000

Welcome
Ms. Carrillo and Ms. Kelnhofer

Song
Ms. Crespo, Ms. Burgos, and Mr. Rodriguez

Student Readings
(Second and third grades)

Presentation of Certificates
Mr. Patterson and Ms. Hernández

View Student Writing Samples

Ice Cream and Cake

Sample Agenda

**El Club de Lectura
End of Year Celebration
May 21, 2002**

Welcome
Lymari (English and Spanish)

- We are proud of how hard you have worked.
- Look at how much better you can read and write now.
- Let's have a party to celebrate your progress!

Play
Dragon: Sol María
Philippa: Julia
Maestra: Lymari
Narradora: Diana
Niñas: Myrta, Kathy

Presentation of Certificates
Mr. Patterson and Ms. Hernández

View Student Writing Samples

Ice Cream and Cake

REFERENCES

Avery, C. 1999. *And with a light touch.* . . . 2nd ed. Portsmouth, NH: Heinemann.

Boehm, R., C. Hoone, T. McGowan, M. McKinney-Browning, O. Miramontes, and P. Porter. 2000a. *States and regions. Grade 4 social studies.* New York: Harcourt Brace.

———. 2000b. *United States. Grade 5 social studies.* New York: Harcourt Brace.

Brown, M. 1949. *The important book.* New York: Harper & Row.

Burns, P., and B. Roe. 2002. *Informal reading inventory: Preprimer to twelfth grade.* Boston: Houghton Mifflin.

Clay, M. 1985. *The early detection of reading difficulties.* Portsmouth, NH: Heinemann.

Cunningham, P. 1995. *Phonics they use: Words for reading and writing.* 2nd ed. New York: HarperCollins.

Cunningham, P., S. A. Moore, J. Cunningham, and D. Moore. 2000. *Reading and writing in elementary classrooms.* New York: Longman.

Flynt, S., and R. Cooter. 1998. *Reading inventory for the classroom.* Boston: Prentice Hall.

Fountas, I., and G. S. Pinnell. 1996. *Guided reading: Good first teaching for all children.* Portsmouth, NH: Heinemann.

Graves, D. 1994. *A fresh look at writing.* Portsmouth, NH: Heinemann.

Henn-Reinke, K. 2001. Club de Lectura: An oasis for struggling readers in bilingual classrooms. *MinneTESOL Journal* 18: 1–11.

Jensen, E. 1998a. *Introduction to brain-compatible learning.* San Diego, CA: Brain Store.

Jensen, E. 1998b. *Teaching with the brain in mind.* Alexandria, VA: Association for Supervision and Curriculum Development.

Johns, J. *Jerry Johns informal reading inventory. (Early literacy assessments and teaching strategies).* Dubuque, IA: Kendall/Hunt.

Leslie, L., and J. Caldwell. 2001. *Qualitative reading instruction.* 3rd ed.. New York: Pearson Allyn and Bacon.

No Child Left Behind Act of 2001. 2001. Conference Report to Accompany H.R. 1, Report No. 107-334, House of Representatives, 107th Congress, 1st session.

Rhodes, L. 1993. *Literacy assessment: A handbook of instruments.* Portsmouth, NH: Heinemann.

Routman, R. 2000. *Conversations: Strategies for teaching, learning, and evaluating.* Portsmouth, NH: Heinemann.

Sparks, J. E. 1982. *Write for power.* Los Angeles: Communication Associates.

Stieglitz, E. 2002. *The Stieglitz Informal Reading Inventory: Assessing reading behaviors from emergent to advanced levels.* Boston: Allyn and Bacon.

Wilde, S., ed. 1996. *Notes from a kid watcher: Selected writings of Yetta M. Goodman.* Portsmouth, NH: Heinemann.

INDEX

ABOUT THE AUTHOR

Kathryn Henn-Reinke (B.A in Spanish, Dominican College, Racine, WI; M.A. in reading, Cardinal Stritch University, Milwaukee, WI; Ph.D. in urban education, University of Wisconsin–Milwaukee) has devoted her career to working with English-language learners (ELLs) and is currently an associate professor of ESL and bilingual education in the Curriculum and Instruction Department at the University of Wisconsin–Oshkosh. Her work centers around first- and second-language literacy development and assessment, and bilingual education.